The Best
Christmas
Programs
for All Ages

Plays, Poems, and Ideas for a Joyful Celebration!

Standard®
PUBLISHING

Cincinnati, Ohio

Scripture taken from the *HOLY BIBLE, NEW INTERNATIONAL VERSION*®. *NIV*®. Copyright © 1973, 1978, 1984 by Biblica, Inc.™ Used by permission of Zondervan. All rights reserved.

Text appeared previously in *Christmas Programs for Children, Standard Christmas Program Book,* and *Christmas Programs for the Church,* © 2003, 2004, 2005, 2006, 2007 by Standard Publishing.

Compiled by: Elaina Meyers
Cover design: Sandra S. Wimmer
Inside design: Bob Korth

Published by Standard Publishing
Cincinnati, Ohio
www.standardpub.com

ISBN 978-0-7847-3307-3

17 16 15 14 13 12   2 3 4 5 6 7 8 9 10

Contents

Poems and Readings for Children

Saying Merry Christmas
Margaret Primrose

Saying Merry Christmas
   Is very easy to do
Because that's what I wish
   For you and you and you.
(Points to audience.)

That Night
Mary Ann Green

The star was ever so bright
Over the stable that night.

Oh, So Small
Mary Ann Green

The Baby, oh, so small
Slept in the cattle stall.

I Would
Mary Ann Green

If I could have been there
I would have bowed with care.
   (Child bows.)

And I would have loved the star
That guided men from afar.
   (Child points to sky.)

Wouldn't it have been great to see
The Baby born for even me?
   (Child points to self.)

Your Christmas Gift
David A. Olds

We're glad you came;
   We have your gift.
We think your heart
   It will uplift.

No, it's not fruit,
   And it's not in a box;
It's not a shirt,
   And it's not socks.

So, spread your arms
   And open your heart;
Here's a hug
   From our shopper's cart.

A Child
Dolores Steger

A Child is born to us this night,
A Child of goodness, love, and light.
A Child whom God has sent to bring
Hope, living, as a Savior King.

I Just Can't Wait for Christmas
Dolores Steger

"I just can't wait for Christmas."
    That's what I hear people say.
But I don't have to wait 'cause
    I praise His birth every day.

A Birthday Celebration
Dolores Steger

A birthday celebration
    We're planning for the day,
When so many years ago
    God sent His Son our way.

A birthday celebration
    Is why there's all the fuss;
A birthday celebration
    For the Savior born to us.

Where Are All the Wise Men?
Dolores Steger

Where are all the wise men? Following the star
To the town called Bethlehem, traveling so far
To adore a Baby, born the King of kings.
See the gifts of love divine that each one of them brings.
Where are all the wise men? They're within our sight.
They're the ones who gather here to celebrate this night.

May Christmas Bring
Dolores Steger

May church bells ring,
Let choirs sing
The glory of the newborn King.
May love and peace this
    Christmas bring.

Christmas Wonder
Amy Houts

Oh, the wonder of it all!
Mary hears the angel call.
Elizabeth and Mary pray,
"Your will, Lord, for us today."

Oh, the wonder of it all!
A baby in the manger stall.
Shepherds, wise men, angels sing
Glory to the newborn King!

May I?
Margaret Primrose

Little stranger in a manger,
    May I sing to You?
May I hold Your tiny hand
    And listen to You coo?

May I kneel beside your bed
    And offer You my heart?
You are precious, very precious,
    And we're friends who will
        never part.

A Gift From the Heart
Cora M. Owen

A gift of love from God's own heart,
    Was His beloved Son.
A gift well-planned right from the start,
    A very precious one.

A gift of love from His great heart,
    Was given freely then.
When Jesus left His home above,
    To save us all. Amen.

Why Not?
Margaret Primrose

Bells ring; choirs sing;
    Christmas will soon be here.
Candles glow; children know
    A special day is near.

Best of all, for great or small,
    Jesus came to earth,
So why not pray every day
    And thank God for His birth?

What Giving!
Cora M. Owen

What a depth of giving!
    When God gave us His best.
What a great example!
    He gave the costliest.

What a gift bestowing,
    When God gave us His Son!
What favor was conferring:
    God gave a Holy One!

Christmas Can Be Anywhere
Margaret Primrose

It's Christmas in Grandma's kitchen
    With its turkey and pumpkin pie.
It's Christmas on the freeway
    And wherever we choose to fly.

It's Christmas in the dusty desert,
    In the lakeside cottage or mall.
It can come to a village church
    As well as a cattle stall.

We can feel the joy of Christmas
    As we push a grocery cart.
Wherever I am, it is Christmas
    Because Jesus is in my heart.

The Reason I'm Glad
Margaret Primrose

When someone reads the story
  Of the Baby in the manger,
I'm very, very glad
  That to me He is no stranger.

For I've given my heart to Jesus,
  And His I'll always be.
There really is no other
  Who could mean as much to me.

I Love Christmas
Margaret Primrose

*(Background sounds of Ea-aw, Ea-aw,
Ea-aw, Moo, Moo, Moo, Baa, Baa,
Baa.)*

I hear the barnyard cries
  The night that Jesus was born;
I feel the scratchy hay
  That would make me wish for morn.

*(Background sounds of bells, carolers,
and muted voices.)*

I hear the sounds of carolers
  And shoppers in the mall.
Then I think of the newborn Baby
  And I really love it all.

Angels, Go
Dolores Steger

Angel, go to Mary.
  Tell her of God's plan.
Let her know that she will bear
  A babe, the Son of man.

Angel, go to Joseph.
  Tell what is to be:
The miracle of Jesus' birth,
  As he sleeps dreamily.

Angel, go to shepherds.
  Tell them to have no fear.
Send them on to Bethlehem,
  The Savior's come; He's here.

Renewal of Christmas
Cora M. Owen

There is renewed faith
  In the message it brings.
When we hear of Christ,
  How our faith to Him clings!

There is renewed hope
  In its promises seen
For our future life;
  Oh, how bright is its sheen!

There is renewed joy
  In its miracle sweet,
Salvation to earth—
  Christ the Savior we greet!

Why Jesus Came

Margaret Primrose

(For a girl in an angel costume.)

I'm really not one of the angels
   Who appeared to some
     shepherds one night.
I didn't hear heavenly music
   While the hillside was circled
     with light.

Yet I'm ready to share the good
   news
   That a Baby who slept in a stall
Was really the Son of God,
   Who came to save us all.

My Gift to Jesus

Margaret Primrose

What can I give to Jesus?
   He doesn't need my bed,
And He can't use the warm blue
   cap
   I sometimes wear on my head.

But here's a toy I bought
   For some child's Christmas gift,
And if my neighbor needs a ride
   My bike will give him a lift.

For what I do for others
   Is a gift for Jesus too.
That's what the Bible tells me,
   And I know God's Word is true.

The Message

Cora M. Owen

The message was so soft and sweet,
   Sent ringing through the night,
While a bright star was shining down,
   To lend the earth its light.

The message was for everyone:
   "A Savior has been born."
"Peace on the earth," the angels sang,
   God's glory to adorn.

The message was a song of praise,
   To welcome God's own Son,
And bringing joy to all the earth,
   Announce the Holy One.

The Christmas Song
Lisamarie Leto

Christmas is a happy time,
For a little kid like me
To celebrate the birthday of
The King from Galilee,
And share the joy of His great love,
Telling children, everywhere
About my heavenly Father
And His tender, precious care.
As I gather with my family and friends,
To happily sing songs of praise
Unto the Lord, with gratefulness,
On this special holiday.
I think about my childhood blessings,
And all that I have too,
And how my Lord has cared for me,
My entire youthful lifetime through.
It's not about the many toys, or
Presents that I can get;
But, being like my Father,
His great goodness to reflect.
To have my heart so filled with
His great presence in every way
Is the greatest gift that a little
   kid can get
On this very special day.

The Legend of the Christmas Spider
Amy Houts

A spider spun a spider's web
upon a Christmas tree.
"This is my gift, my humble gift,
I give for you, from me."
It shimmered and it glistened,
the spider's glossy shroud.
The children looked in wonder.
The tree stood tall and proud.
Did you know the tinsel
we place so carefully
came from the sparkling spider's
   web
that clothed the Christmas tree?

Before Her

Mary Ann Green

A figure appeared before her
And her heart began to stir.

"Be not afraid," he said.
She humbly bowed her head.

"The Christ child's mother you will be,
For God has found favor with thee."

"Oh, but this cannot be;
I'm not married you see."

"Joseph will take you as his bride
And stand as husband by your side."

"Then the Christ child's mother I will be,
For it is God's will I seek for me."

Then the man disappeared
And Mary no longer feared.

She quietly pondered in her heart
How in God's plan she had a part.

In awe she spoke aloud:
"I will carry the Christ child."

Holiday Puzzle
Lisamarie Leto

At this special and holy time of the year,
We reflect upon **C**hrist's goodness and His love,
Given so wonderfully and abundantly from
The precious **H**eaven above.
Thankful are we for His **R**ighteousness,
And His **I**ncredible grace and care,
His **S**piritual guidance and mercy,
And for always being there.
Grateful are we for His **T**errific friendship,
And for being a Father so true;
For His **M**agnificent, **A**ll-powerful presence,
In everything that we do.
This is a **S**acred holiday,
Filled with joy and happiness from the start.
Put together the underlined, capital letters,
And discover the holiday of which
Christ is the heart!

CHRISTMAS

Look Upon the Child
Dolores Steger

Born to be a King of kings,
Born as Savior of the earth.
Now we look upon this Child
And celebrate this day His birth.

A Time to Celebrate

Margaret Primrose

OLDER CHILD:	Whether we're big
YOUNGER CHILD:	Or whether we're small,
MIDDLE CHILD:	Christmas is special for one and all.
TWO GIRLS:	Whether we're girls
TWO BOYS:	Or whether we're boys,
TWO GIRLS AND TWO BOYS:	Christmas means more than games and toys.
A BOY:	It's a time to give;
A GIRL:	It's a time to sing
ALL:	Our song of praise to the newborn King.

(May be followed with a carol.)

A Present for Jesus

Margaret Primrose

FIRST CHILD:

There are presents for Mother and Daddy and me,
And they all look pretty under the tree,
But not one for Jesus do I ever see.
I want Him to have one, but what could it be?

SECOND CHILD:
(Carries a Bible.)

"That's very simple," my mom said to me.
"It's here in God's Book for all to see."
We give Him a gift when we do a good deed,
So why don't we give to someone in need?
(Read from Matthew 25:40.)

FIRST CHILD:

Thanks for your time in telling me so.
That's what I really wanted to know.
I'll use my allowance to buy a toy
And give it to some needy girl or boy.

A Welcome
Dolores Steger

The birthday is here
   Of our Savior so dear.
May our program please you
   And the Lord Jesus too.

Cherub
Dolores Steger

I am a little cherub,
   And I am here to say,
Blessings, peace be with you,
   On this Christmas day.

Baby Savior
Dolores Steger

Baby Savior, baby king,
   Magi, gifts are offering
To You, Savior, baby king
   For the gifts to us You bring.

Christ Abides
Dolores Steger

Christ abides in a manger,
   The place where peace and
      hope start;
Christ abides in a manger,
   And always within my heart.

The Christ Who's in Christmas
Dolores Steger

May your days all be merry,
   And may they be bright
With the Christ who's in
      Christmas
   As your guiding light.

The Birthday Cake
Dolores Steger

Blend a lot of joyfulness
   With a dash of cheer;
Stir in scads of happiness,
   Enough to last all year.
Mix in cups and cups of love
   And then, with caring, bake
This tribute to the newborn king:
   A happy birthday cake.

Watching and Waiting
Dolores Steger

Watching and waiting,
   Oh, Christmas draws near,
And with it the coming
   Of Jesus so dear.

Watching and waiting,
   I do it each year,
But praise to the Lord,
   He is already here.

A Baby Is Sleeping

Dolores Steger

A baby is sleeping in manger, on hay,
While shepherds and others adore Him this day;
A baby is waking, He'll rise and He'll bring
The promise to all of a Savior and king.

In a Stable

Dolores Steger

In a stable, silently,
The friendly beasts look on to see
A babe born for eternity.

In a stable, all around,
Angel choirs are there found,
Hear their "Alleluia" sound.

In a stable, all about,
Shepherds show they have no doubt,
"We've seen the Lord of lords!" they shout.

In a stable far away,
All in adoration pray
And praise the Child on Christmas Day.

Clear in Sight

Dolores Steger

Here's hoping your Christmas is merry and bright,
Beginning at dawn to the darkness of night;
So herald the birthday with joy and delight
By keeping the Lord Jesus clear in your sight.

We Present
Cora M. Owen

We present a child to you,
Who came to earth God's will to do.
His name is Jesus, precious one.
Beloved of God, He is His Son.

We point to a manger bed,
Where the Savior laid His head.
It was there on bed of hay,
Christ was born on Christmas day.

On a Bright and Starry Night
Cora M. Owen

On a bright and starry night,
    Shepherds on a quiet hill,
Keeping watch over their sheep,
    Then their souls received a
        thrill.

Angels' singing filled the air.
    Voices sounding oh, so sweet,
Told them to go to Bethlehem,
    Infant Jesus Christ to meet.

Hurriedly, they came to town,
    To a lowly manger bed,
Where they found the precious
        babe,
    Then the joyful news they spread.

A Christmas Song
Dolores Steger

Oh, sing a little Christmas song,
    A little melody
Of angels and of shepherds
    Who hurried there to see,
Of friendly beasts, of Mary,
    Of Joseph by a stall,
Of Jesus sleeping peacefully,
    Surrounded by them all;
Oh, sing a little Christmas song,
    A little melody,
And praise our God who sent His
        Son
    For all eternity.

The Perfect Gift
Cora M. Owen

At Christmastime we make a
        search,
    For gifts that are just right,
For all our family and friends,
    To make their Christmas bright.

God has given a perfect Gift.
    It's meant for everyone.
He sent Him down so long ago
    His own beloved Son.

It is a gift that's always right,
    Salvation through this One.
And it will last eternally.
    God's gift can't be outdone.

Where Did It Go?
Donna Nevling

Tell me, where did it go, that
   lovely brilliant star,
That so very long ago led wise
   men from afar?
Did it just melt away and fall
   down from the sky,
Or did it shrink so small, it can't
   be seen by human eye?

Oh, no, it grew much bigger and
   it's closer to us now.
It shines right through the hearts
   of all who humbly bow,
And offer to the Savior the gift of
   their hearts,
For anywhere His throne is, His
   light He will impart!

It's Christmas Now
Dolores Steger

I hear the angels as they sing;
What wondrous news it is they
   bring,
A message of a newborn King.

I see the shepherds, wise men go
To see the babe so sweet and low,
Then spread the word of all they
   know.

I feel the hope in Him somehow,
And I, like those before me, bow
To Him; oh, joy, it's Christmas now.

God's Christmas Tree
Donna Nevling

When it's Christmastime, there
   are such lovely sights.
I like most of all to look at all the
   lights.
But when the silver lamps
   against the velvet sky I see,
I think there's nothing lovelier
   than God's Christmas tree!

All Is Well
Cora M. Owen

Jesus came and all is well,
Came to this old world to dwell.
To a people lost in sin,
Bringing hope and peace within.
So we choose to celebrate the
Birthday of this one so great.
On this day we want to tell,
Jesus came and all is well.

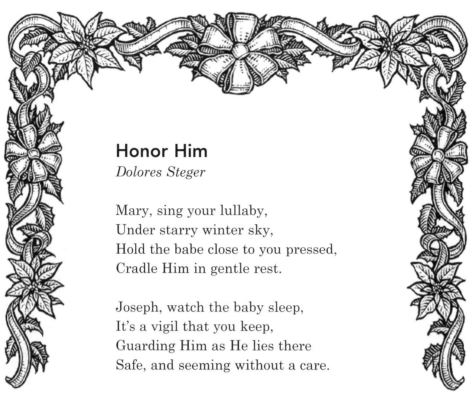

Honor Him

Dolores Steger

Mary, sing your lullaby,
Under starry winter sky,
Hold the babe close to you pressed,
Cradle Him in gentle rest.

Joseph, watch the baby sleep,
It's a vigil that you keep,
Guarding Him as He lies there
Safe, and seeming without a care.

Shepherds who are listening
To the message angels bring,
Knowing what you've seen and heard,
Go at once and spread the word.

Wise men with the gifts you bear,
Follow the star to the house where
You'll present them with great joy
To the King, a little boy.

Angels in the realms above,
Touch Him with eternal love,
'Round Him gather, never cease
To enfold Him in your peace.

People, at this time, behold
The promise that was made of old.
Then evermore through all your days
Honor Him with all your praise.

Why Did He Come?
Cora M. Owen

Why was Christ willing to come to earth,
With such a humble and lowly birth?
He came to us because of His grace.
Born so poor as He came to this place.

He became poor that we might be rich.
Laid aside glory for this world's niche.
Gave up His throne in Heaven above,
That He could show us His Father's love.

All Is Now Quiet
Dolores Steger

All is now quiet in Bethlehem town,
   To Heaven the angels returned.
The shepherds departed to spread the good news
   Of the tidings so true they have learned;
The Magi are gone to their Orient homes,
   Remembering those blessed things
They saw and they heard, as they worshiped a babe
   Whom they knew as the king of kings;
All is now quiet in Bethlehem town,
   The prophecies have proven true;
The Savior is born and He lives, oh, He lives
   In hearts, both of me and of you.

They Say

Dolores Steger

Joseph says: "One night I slept
   And in my dreams an angel came
To tell me Mary's child, a son,
   Is to have Jesus as His name."

Mary says: "From God I know
   I soon will give birth to a son,
A child to reign eternally
   As king and as God's chosen one."

Angels say: "The Christ is born,
   So, shepherds, go to Bethlehem,
Find Mary, Joseph, and the babe,
   And leave your sheep to honor them."

Shepherds say: "We've seen the child
   And we have no more time to lose,
To spread the word He is the Lord,
   The world should hear of our good news."

Herod says: "Who is this child
   That all the people talk about?
Is He a king who'll pose a threat?
   I'll ask the wise men to find out."

Wise men say: "We've brought our gifts
   Unto the king this very day.
We won't tell Herod where He is,
   We'll go home by another way."

Joseph says: "We'll rear this Child."
   Mary says: "He'll grow to be
The Lord of lords, the King of kings."
   And shepherds, wise men, all agree.

Celebrate the Birth
Lillian Robbins

Christmas Eve is such an exciting time,
　Mixed feelings just take control.
My mom says it's always the same
　Ever since the days of old.

I want to sleep so tomorrow will come,
　But I just can't settle down.
I keep thinking about our Christmas gifts,
　Lighted trees that cover our town.

Christmas brings light and color to life,
　And fills each heart with joy.
Children think it's just all about toys
　Brought to all the girls and boys.

There is really more for us, you know,
　The things that always last.
Like love and peace God brings to all.
　That's real and won't just pass.

God promised to send the living Christ
　To save us for Heaven above.
It all came to be on that holy night,
　In Jesus, God's dearest love.

We're impatient to wait for early dawn,
　Our toys and gifts to receive.
But the best gift of all is freely given.
　In Jesus we must believe.

May this be a happy Christmastime
　And the joys of life be found.
Celebrate the birth of Jesus the Christ
　As the blessings of God abound.

Christmas Morn
Dolores Steger

On Christmas Eve in bed I'll be.
I'll close my eyes and there I'll see
a vision—the nativity.

The stars glow in the heavens where
they shine on stable cold and bare.
A babe rests, tender, sleeping there.

An angel band, their trumpets play
while shepherds come to honor, pray,
and wise men bring their gifts array.

I wake on Christmas morn to find
the scene still in my heart and mind
and praise the Child sent to mankind.

Reporting the News
Cora M. Owen

The angels first reported the news,
    Of the Messiah's birth.
Announcing it to shepherds of old,
    Telling of peace on earth.

The shepherds then reported the news,
    After a visit to
The manger bed of Jesus Christ.
    The Savior they came to view.

I am reporting the news to you.
    A Savior has been born.
One who brought salvation to earth,
    Long ago on Christmas morn.

Jesus' Birth

Dolores Steger

When fireplaces glow with embers
in the coldness of Decembers,
warmth descends upon the earth
as peace, love, hope in Jesus' birth.

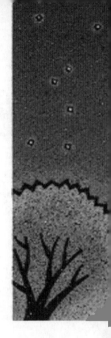

In Humility

Lillian Robbins

There was no smooth road
Nor comfortable ride
  To travel the Bethlehem way.

Travelers made their way
As best they could,
  Chilled nights or heat of day.

The distance was long
As Joseph knew well,
  But what could he do but go?

All the world should be taxed
Caesar Augustus decreed.
  No compassion at all would he
  show.

The donkey was made ready
For Mary to ride
  Though her baby would be born
  soon.

They didn't really know
Whether midnight or morning
  Or even in the heat of noon.

Of the lineage of David,
They had no choice
  But to go to the Bethlehem town.

With hope in their hearts
And prayer on their lips,
  Lodging must surely be found.

Many others had come;
Rooms had been taken,
  Not a place they could have slept.

But a stable was near;
It was offered to them,
  Just a shelter where animals
  were kept.

Would Joseph even dare
To take Mary his wife
  To such a lowly abode?

Would pride take preeminence
Over what must be done?
  Or would humility surely be
    showed?

They settled for the night
As best they could
  To rest on a bed of straw.

Together they shared
As Jesus came to earth.
  Though others never even saw.

A baby's quiet cry,
A mother's loving arms,
  And Joseph who stayed near by.

The wondrous sound came
In a baby's wee voice.
  In a manger He was destined to lie.

In humility He was born
In a cattle stall
  To live on earth among men.

His mission in life
For all the world
  Was to save us from our sin.

What a glorious gift
God sent from above,
  More wondrous than we even
    can know.

But it was all for us
Wherever we are.
  His compassionate love did He
    show.

Let's all thank God
For His unspeakable gift
  That can never be compared.

By God's great might,
His response to sin;
  His love for us He shared.

We wish for all of you a godly
  Christmas.

Poems and Readings for Children

The Colors of Christmas

Cora M. Owen

The color of Christmas is golden,
  Like the lovely shining star
That shone on the path of the wise men,
  As they traveled from afar.

The color of Christmas is silver,
  Like the tinsel on the tree
That sparkles with its decorations.
  It gives us pleasure to see.

The color of Christmas is scarlet
  Seen in our bright Christmas bows,
And lights shining forth from the windows.
  Oh, how they shimmer and glow.

The color of Christmas is emerald
  Just take a look at the tree.
It symbolizes eternal life
  That God offers you and me.

I love all the colors of Christmas,
  Red and silver, gold and green.
They make a most radiant picture,
  Bringing much joy to the scene.

Enjoy
by Dolores Steger

Enjoy each gift, each card, each toy.
But, then, with happiness and joy,
Shout praises for the Christ Child boy.

Born for You and Me
by Dolores Steger

Let every Christmas ornament
On every Christmas tree
Remind me of the Savior
Born for you and me.

Twinkle, Twinkle
by Dolores Steger

Twinkle, twinkle little star.
Shine on manger bed
Where the baby, Jesus, child
Rests His kingly head.

Happy Birthday
by Dolores Steger

Baby Jesus, little one,
We all know You are God's Son.
And on this, Your special day,
Happy Birthday's what we say!

Why?

by Dolores Steger

Why a stable cold and bare?
It's God's hand that placed Him there.
Why the angels all about?
It's the good news. Hear them shout!
Why the shepherds in that place?
They came to see His holy face.
Why the wise men from afar?
They've been guided by a star.
Why the child, asleep, I see?
Savior, King of kings, He'll be.

Are You Wise?

by Kenton K. Smith

How do you know if you are wise?
Must your brain be of greater-than-average size?
Must you read 300 books in a year,
And quote them to anyone willing to hear?
Must you earn for yourself a PhD
From a reputable university?
Must you use words of ponderous size,
Like *philanthropy* or *philosophize*?
Do you give up? Then here is a clue:
Wise men still seek Him—do you?

Wise Men

(a rhyme for three children)
by Dolores Steger

CHILD 1: I am a wise man, and I have been told
A baby king's born. And I bring Him
some gold.

CHILD 2: I am a wise man and, just for the king,
It's sweet-smelling incense that to Him
I bring.

CHILD 3: I am a wise man and myrrh
that's so mild
Is what I will give to that
most special child.

ALL: We are three wise men with gifts rare and new.
Will you, with all honor, bring gifts for Him too?

Poems and Readings for Children

C-H-R-I-S-T-M-A-S

by Alyce Pickett

Summary: A poetic reading about the reason we celebrate the holiday season.

Characters:

9 children with speaking parts

Props: 9 pieces of poster board, each with a letter of the word *Christmas*

Children walk on stage, each holding a letter. When in place, children hold the letters in front of them to spell CHRISTMAS.

C: is for Christ child . . . Jesus was His name.

H: is for Heaven, His home before He came.

R: our Redeemer, born in a stable dim,

I: is the inn that had no room for Him.

S: is the star showing men the way.

T: is tidings shepherds heard that day.

M: is mother of the child born that night,

A: is angels who came in shining bright,

S: is for Savior . . . the one God sent to give light.

[Blackout.]

I Can Plainly See

(a verse for five children)
by Dolores Steger

CHILD 1:   I am just a little lamb,
            But I can plainly see
            A baby in a manger,
            Lying nearby me.

CHILD 2:   I'm just a little donkey,
            But I can plainly see
            A Lord there in the manger,
            Born to set men free.

CHILD 3:   I am just a little cow,
            But I can plainly see
            A prince there in the manger,
            Sleeping peacefully.

CHILD 4:   I am just a little camel,
            But I can plainly see
            A king there in a manger.
            A King of kings is He.

CHILD 5:   I am just a little dove,
            But I can plainly see
            A Savior in a manger
            Who'll live eternally.

Skits and Plays for Children

Wish List

by JOHN COSPER

Summary: A little girl remembers how Christmas used to be all about getting gifts, until she learned the true spirit is giving.

Character:

GIRL—young girl appearing to look about 4 or 5

Setting: bare stage

Costume: modern-day little girl's clothing

GIRL: When I was a really littler kid, there was only one thing I wanted for Christmas: a dollie! I begged my mommy and daddy until I got her.

But then you know what happened? I grew up. Yup, and when I was about, mmmmm, 4, I wanted a grown-up present. I wanted a Pink Pretty Princess Super Bike 2000. All year long, I begged my mommy and daddy for the bike, and guess what? I got it! And I got out and saw the world.

But then, a long time later, when I was about, oh, 6, I learned about a present even better than a bike, or a dollie. I heard about it in church. I also learned it was the very first and bestest Christmas present ever. Know what it was? It was a baby, but not like my dollie. It was a real one, and His name was Jesus. He was God's only Son. I asked my mommy and daddy for Jesus, but this time, they told me I had to ask Jesus himself to come into my heart. And you know what? He did! Yup! *[knocks on chest]* He's right in there. He keeps me company all day.

But you know what? It's been a year since I got Jesus, and there's still one more thing I want for Christmas. See, I've been hearing that there are kids in the world that don't know about Jesus. Matter of fact, there are some kids in the world that have never heard about Christmas.

So I asked my mommy and my daddy, and you know what they said? They said Jesus was a gift that only I could give. Jesus wants me to tell everyone I know about Him. Can you believe that? I told them they were crazy, but then I got to thinking. Now I have Jesus, and now, I can go and tell everyone that Jesus loves them.

[Blackout.]

No Jesus, No Christmas

by BRETT PARKER

Summary: Everyone in the Taylor family is getting ready to go see Santa at the mall! The only problem is that the family is taking a little bit longer to get ready than MR. TAYLOR expected.

Characters:

MR. TAYLOR—middle-aged man, a little high-strung, best if played by a teen or adult

MRS. TAYLOR—middle-aged woman, calm and cheerful, best if played by a teen or adult

JASON—boy about 8 years old, brother of ASHLEY

ASHLEY—girl about 6 years old, sister of JASON

Setting: living room of the Taylor family home

Props: a plate or tray for Christmas cookies, newspaper, coffee mug, a watch, small living room table and seats for 4, a roll of paper or a long piece of paper for a Christmas list, a coat

Costumes: modern-day clothing

The skit opens with MR. TAYLOR waltzing into the living room, coffee mug in hand, cheerfully whistling to the tune of "Jingle Bells." He sits down in his chair, picks up the newspaper and begins to read it. After a moment he glances at his watch. He is shocked to realize what time it is. He runs over to the side and appears to be looking out a window.

MR. TAYLOR: Oh no! That snow is really coming down! We've got to get going! *[He looks around and notices that no one else is in the room with him. He walks to back of the room and looks up the staircase.]* Honey? Kids? Hurry up! If we don't leave soon we're going to miss Santa!

[MRS. TAYLOR enters living room carrying a plate of Christmas cookies and sets them down on a small table in the middle of the room.]

MRS. TAYLOR: Oh relax, dear. Santa will be at the mall all day long. I'm sure everyone will get a chance to see him.

MR. TAYLOR: Not at this pace. *[He glances at his watch again.]* By the time we fight through traffic in the snow to get to the mall, Santa will probably be on his lunch break. And you know it's only a few days before Christmas. Who knows how long the line to see him will be after that?

MRS. TAYLOR: Now, dear. Please just be calm. You know how excited the kids are to see Santa. I'm sure they don't mind the traffic or waiting in the lines.

MR. TAYLOR: Yes, but I do. *[pauses for a moment, and then notices that the kids are still not anywhere to be seen]* Jason! Ashley! Let's go!

[JASON enters the room running, jumping and acting completely wild.]

JASON: Yippee! Santa, here I come! This is going to be great! I've been looking forward to this for a whole year!

MRS. TAYLOR: *[laughing at JASON's enthusiasm]* Well, I'm glad you're excited! Do you know what you're going to ask Santa for Christmas?

JASON: *[his eyes get wide and a huge smile comes across his face]* Do I? You better believe I do! I've got it all figured out, Mom. I'm asking Santa for the new, the awesome, Super Power Space Soldier action figure, complete with a laser gun, turbo charged utility belt, and his own personal spaceship! Not only that, but he is able to leap, run, crawl, jump, fly and perform Ninja moves! *[He lets out a loud Ninja scream and starts karate chopping MR. TAYLOR.]*

MR. TAYLOR: Yeah, yeah. Well, Sport, if we don't hurry you won't get a chance to tell Santa anything. Where's your sister? *[loudly]* Ashley?

ASHLEY: *[She happily skips into room, singing "Santa Claus Is Coming to Town." She has with her a large roll of paper; singing with different lyrics]* He sees me when I'm sleeping, he knows when I'm awake! He knows if *I've* been bad or good, and *I have* been good for goodness sake!

MR. TAYLOR: There you are, Ashley. Are you ready? What took you so long?

ASHLEY: Well, of course I'm ready *now*, Daddy. I couldn't leave before I finished writing my Christmas list to Santa.

MRS. TAYLOR: *[smiling]* And what are *you* asking from Santa this year?

ASHLEY: *[clears her throat]* Well, as you all know, I have been on my best behavior for the last three weeks. I have cleaned my room *everyday*, eaten *all* the food on my dinner plate each night—even the broccoli— and I even helped my teacher erase the board last week. So, because I have been *really* good, I made my list extra long this year. *[She drops*

one end of the roll of paper, her list, and lets it roll across the room.
Everyone is astonished to see how long her list is.]

MRS. TAYLOR: My, that certainly looks like a long list, Ashley.

MR. TAYLOR: Come on, Ashley. You can read it to us in the car. The snow
is coming down really hard now.

JASON: Yeah! We don't have time, now! We're going to miss . . .

ASHLEY: *[interrupts JASON]* First, I am asking for the new Jet Ski Barbie.
Next, I would like a new pink lunch box, complete with thermos,
handle, and cup holder. I also want a make-up kit, and nurse's kit,
a sled, a new hairbrush, an easy-bake oven, a cotton candy machine,
a bubblegum machine, a doll house, a pony, a puppy, a kitten, *two*
bunny rabbits, a gold-fish and a turtle.

MRS. TAYLOR: *[somewhat disappointed]* Goodness, that *IS* quite a long
list, sweetie. Are you sure you need all of those things?

JASON: Honestly Ashley, what are you trying to do? Turn our house into a
zoo?

ASHLEY: We might as well. Your room is already a pig sty! *[She rubs her
knuckles on his head and begins to run away, laughing]*

JASON: *[chases after ASHLEY]* Is not!

ASHLEY: Is too! *[makes pig sounds]*

MR. TAYLOR: *[becoming upset]* Hey! We DO NOT have time for this! Now
I'm going to go start the car, and when I get back everyone had better
be friendly and ready to go! *[puts on his coat and then exits]*

JASON: *[chases ASHLEY again]* Is not times one hundred!

ASHLEY: Is too times one million!

JASON: Is not times a gazillion!

ASHLEY: That's not even a real number!

JASON: Is too!

ASHLEY: Is not!

MRS. TAYLOR: Please, kids. Try to be nice to each other. It's Christmastime. *[walking over to look outside]* Wow. It really is snowing hard!
[sees MR. TAYLOR coming back] Here comes your dad.

*[JASON and ASHLEY quit chasing each other and try to look like they are
getting ready. MR. TAYLOR quickly enters. He shivers and takes off his coat.
He has a look of disappointment on his face]*

MR. TAYLOR: Well, everyone, I am afraid I have some bad news. It looks
like we are snowed in.

JASON: What?

ASHLEY: Isn't there anything we can do?

MR. TAYLOR: I'm sorry, kids. There's just too much snow. I can't even get the car out of the driveway. It looks like we're stuck here for a while. At least until the roads clear up.

MRS. TAYLOR: Oh, dear. I'm so sorry everyone.

JASON: No Santa?

MR. TAYLOR: I'm afraid not, Jason.

JASON: Without telling Santa what I want, he'll never know what to bring me! That means no Santa, no Christmas. *[turns to ASHLEY]* This is all your fault! If you wouldn't have taken so long with your Christmas list, we could have gotten to see Santa!

ASHLEY: My fault? *[stuttering]* Why . . . I have never in all my life . . . How rude!

MR. TAYLOR: Hey! *[becoming angry again]* What did I say about arguing? There will be no arguing! This is becoming a very stressful day!

MRS. TAYLOR: Dear, please, calm down. Have a seat. *[motions for MR. TAYLOR to sit in his chair]* Jason, Ashley. You too. Sit, sit. *[waits for everyone to have a seat and puts her hands on her hips]* Does anyone here know the real meaning of Christmas? Have you forgotten what Christmas is really all about?

JASON: Santa?

ASHLEY: Presents?

MRS. TAYLOR: No, it's not about Christmas trees, or going to the mall, Santa, or even presents. *[smiling bright]* It's about Jesus! On Christmas, we celebrate the birth of Jesus. Without him, there wouldn't be a Christmas. It's not "No Santa, no Christmas," Jason. It's "No *Jesus*, no Christmas." We don't need gifts or toys to have Christmas. All we need is Jesus.

MR. TAYLOR: *[realizing that he shouldn't be so angry]* Your mom is right, kids. I think I missed the meaning of Christmas too. I got so wrapped up in getting you guys to the mall to see Santa that I forgot the whole point of Christmas, to celebrate Jesus' birthday. And I am so lucky that I get to celebrate with all of you! I'm sorry that I got so mad and yelled.

ASHLEY: I'm sorry too. I guess my list is a little too long, huh? I don't really need *all* of those things on my list. Christmas shouldn't be about getting a lot of presents.

JASON: Yeah, I forgot what Christmas was about too. I was so set on seeing Santa that I wouldn't let anything get in the way. I'm sorry I was so mean to you, Ashley.

ASHLEY: It's all right, Jason. From now on we should try to be nice to each other. And not because Santa Claus is watching, but because Jesus wants us to.

MRS. TAYLOR: Now that's the Christmas spirit!

MR. TAYLOR: It certainly is! I'm so proud of you two! *[looks at MRS. TAYLOR]* And you too, Mom. Thanks for reminding us what Christmas should really be about. Group hug! *[they all run over to MRS. TAYLOR and engage in a group hug]*

MRS. TAYLOR: Thank you, everyone!

MR. TAYLOR: *[glances outside]* Aw. I still feel bad about the snow, though. How are we going to get these lists to Santa?

MRS. TAYLOR: Why don't we e-mail them to Santa?

JASON: We can do that?

MRS. TAYLOR: Of course we can!

ASHLEY: All right!

JASON: Awesome! *[gives ASHLEY a high five]*

MR. TAYLOR: Come on, kids! I'll help you write them! *[exits, followed by JASON and ASHLEY]*

MRS. TAYLOR: *[looks up]* Happy Birthday, Jesus! *[Exits. Blackout.]*

The Ad Campaign

by JOHN COSPER

Summary: A zealous angel wants to arrange a mass media campaign to announce the birth of Jesus but another explains God's simple plan for revealing Christ to the world.

Characters:
    MICHAEL—angel
    DARRELL—angel

Setting: Heaven

Costumes: angel robes

MICHAEL: Well, Darrell, we're at T-minus 20 hours to the big event. Are you ready?

DARRELL: Ready? I was made for this, pal!

MICHAEL: Weren't we all?

DARRELL: I can't believe the day is here.

MICHAEL: I know. The Son of God is about to enter creation and bridge the gap between God and people!

DARRELL: And we're just the guys to tell the whole world about it!

MICHAEL: You bet we—Wait, what are we gonna do?

DARRELL: Why, kick off the marketing campaign for Jesus, of course!

MICHAEL: What marketing campaign? I never heard anything about this.

DARRELL: Not to worry. I've already mapped the whole thing out. First, we start with the teaser.

MICHAEL: Teaser?

DARRELL: The star, of course. It's just a sample, a taste, a small sign of things to come—something that'll get people talking. Then, after a month or so, we start with the billboards.

MICHAEL: Billboards?

DARRELL: That's right. I'm thinking one or two on every major route in Israel, plus a few extras inside the big cities like Jerusalem. At first, they'll have simple quotes from the prophets. Something like, "To us a child is born!" Maybe with a picture of the star.

MICHAEL: I don't know . . .

DARRELL: You're right. We'll put the baby's picture on the billboards. And once those signs are up, we start with the radio spots.

MICHAEL: Radio spots? What are you talking about?

DARRELL: You're right. No one listens to the radio any more. We'll advertise on television—a 30-second spot in prime time, featuring the angelic host singing of His birth! Of course, once He's old enough to talk, we'll send Him on the chat shows.

MICHAEL: Darrell . . .

DARRELL: Not the smutty shows, though. I'm thinking the legit morning news programs, and maybe one of the prime time shows. Like *60 Minutes*.

MICHAEL: Darrell! Television won't be invented for another two millennia!

DARRELL: So?

MICHAEL: That's gonna be a little late for your little advertising campaign.

DARRELL: Little? Michael, this is no little ad campaign! This is the biggest moment in history since . . . well, since EVER!

MICHAEL: And God's got it all planned out already.

DARRELL: He has?

MICHAEL: Yes.

DARRELL: Well, don't leave me in suspense! What's He got planned? Billboards? Fliers? Or simply a blimp to fly over the colisseum?

MICHAEL: One star and one sign.

DARRELL: And?

MICHAEL: And that's it. One star and one sign.

DARRELL: That's it?

MICHAEL: That's all He needs.

DARRELL: That can't be! What if people aren't around to see the star? What if it's cloudy? And how is everyone going to see one sign?

MICHAEL: Darrell, this is God's Son. He's had a long time to prepare for it. And if the hand that made all creation only needs a star and a sign . . . I'd say He's got everything He needs.

[Blackout.]

Christmas While You Wait

by SUSAN SUNDWALL

Summary: Two days before Christmas, ANNIE and her brother CHUCK discover how meaningful it is to do something special for others while they wait for the big holiday.

Characters:
  ANNIE—9-year-old girl
  CHUCK—ANNIE's 11-year-old brother
  MOM—would work best if played by a teen girl

Setting: two chairs sit center stage in the living room; a Christmas tree is behind them stage left.

Props: two chairs, winter coats, bag of canned goods, sound device for car door slamming, small decorated tree.

Costumes: modern-day clothing

CHUCK sits with his elbows on his knees, his chin in his hands, looking forward as though through a window.

CHUCK: C'mon, c'mon!

ANNIE: *[enters stage right, sits next to CHUCK and looks out]* Bored?

CHUCK: It's two days to Christmas and I just know I'm getting new skis. But we need some snow. Look at that!

ANNIE: *[looks out again]* All I see is . . .

CHUCK: Dead grass and bare trees!

ANNIE: I don't know, Chuck. I kind of like the bare branches against the sky.

CHUCK: *[looks at her, disgusted]* Annie!

ANNIE: *[shrugs]* Sorry, there's nothing I can do to bring snow. I know something that might help though. Remember what the minister said last Sunday? It was all about waiting for Christmas and . . .

MOM: *[calls from off stage]* Annie . . . Chuck! *[rushes in, stage right, wearing winter coat and carrying a bag of canned goods]* There you are! I need some help you two.

ANNIE: What's going on Mom?

Mom: The van is full of bags for the food pantry and Mrs. Gibbons won't be able to help me with it.

Chuck: *[grins and makes a muscle]* I guess I'm your man, Mom.

Annie: What do we have to do?

Mom: We'll take the food to the pantry, unload, and wait for people to pick it up.

Chuck: All that? Oh man, that could take the rest of the afternoon!

Annie: *[snaps her fingers]* That's right. You had a lot of important things *[looking out the window for snow]* to do. Hey, Mom and I can handle it.

Mom: I'd really appreciate the help.

Chuck: Yeah, OK.

Annie: *[makes a muscle, frowns and looks at Chuck]* OK . . . you lift bags and I'll pass stuff out.

Mom: *[exits stage right and calls over her shoulder]* Let's go!

Annie: *[follows Mom]* Dashing through the snow . . . la, la, la.

Chuck: *[gestures to Annie]* Hey, so what about waiting for Christmas . . . *[follows Annie out]*

[Offstage, Annie and Chuck put on winter coats. The stage is empty for about 15 seconds, and then a car door slams offstage.]

Chuck: *[enters stage right, removes coat and plops into chair]* Whew! I'm beat!

Annie: *[enters behind Chuck looking bewildered, removes coat]* Wow, all those people.

Chuck: It was somethin' huh?

Annie: That one little boy only had a sweater, no coat. And it's really cold out.

Chuck: *[grins]* I threw in some extra snacks for him.

Annie: *[smiles at Chuck]* I told his mom about the free turkey list at the church.

Chuck: Hey, that might make their Christmas a little brighter! Nice going Sis!

Annie: Didn't it feel great helping out? The afternoon sure went fast.

Chuck: Sure did. You know, I'm getting pretty hungry myself. I wonder what's for supper.

Mom: *[Enters stage right, brushing off her coat]* You both did such a good job today Dad and I are taking you to Angelo's for supper tonight.

ANNIE: [claps] Wahoo! I love Angelo's. I'll have extra cheese pizza and maybe canoli for dessert.

CHUCK: [stares at MOM, points at her coat] Is that . . .

MOM: [brushes a few more flakes off her shoulder] We'll have to get going though. It's starting to snow pretty hard.

CHUCK: [throws both arms in the air] I knew it! Snow!

MOM: Grab your coats. We'll be waiting in the car. [exits stage right.]

ANNIE: This is going to be the best Christmas! And we did just what the minister said.

CHUCK: [turns to ANNIE] Oh yeah, so what about waiting for Christmas?

ANNIE: [gestures with hands outward] It was real simple; do something for someone else while you wait.

CHUCK: [laughs] It sure beats waiting for snow; that's a real bore.

ANNIE: Waiting to eat, like those people at the pantry, is worse.

CHUCK: Yeah, I'm sure glad we could help. It was a good way to wait.

ANNIE: I hope we don't have to wait too long for our pizza. Oh, and Chuck?

CHUCK: Yeah.

ANNIE: What makes you so sure you're getting skis for Christmas?

CHUCK: I might have seen something in a closet . . .

ANNIE: [gasps, lightly punches his arm and covers her mouth] Oh, you didn't . . .

CHUCK: [raises hands above his head] Something about this long and . . .

ANNIE: You're so bad . . .

[CHUCK and ANNIE exit stage right whispering and giggling about the skis. Blackout.]

From the Manger

by DIXIE PHILLIPS

Summary: A poetic rhythmic reading of the Christmas story.
Characters:
>NARRATOR—would work best if played by a grandparent figure
>DONKEY—male or female
>MARY—mother of Jesus
>JOSEPH—father of Jesus
>INNKEEPER—male, should appear middle-aged
>ANGELS—four are needed, can be male or female
>SHEPHERDS—four are needed, can be male or female
>WISEMEN—three are needed, all males
>THE STAR—female

Setting: A stable setting stage right. NARRATOR opens at center stage. The children's recitations are done center stage and then after reciting their pieces they move to stage right and form a nativity scene for final scene.

Props: a stuffed lamb for SHEPHERD 1, WISEMEN should each have a wrapped gift to present to the baby Jesus, baby doll for baby Jesus, staffs for each SHEPHERD, rocking chair for NARRATOR, music for "Away in a Manger"

Costumes: Bible-times costumes, white robes for ANGELS, silver robe for THE STAR, modern-day dress for NARRATOR

All lines are said in a rhythmic pattern. NARRATOR is sitting in a rocking chair at stage right to indicate he or she is a grandparent sharing the Christmas story.

NARRATOR: The Christmas story never grows old. It's still the greatest story ever told. So you all sit back and enjoy the rhymes told by each girl and boy!

[DONKEY, MARY & JOSEPH enter.]

DONKEY: I am the donkey all fuzzy and brown. I carried Mary to that tiny town. HEEEE HAWWWW!

MARY: Joseph, we must stop right away. This baby will be born today.

JOSEPH: Look! There is an inn up ahead. Maybe they will have a room and bed.

[JOSEPH pretends to knock on door.]

INNKEEPER: We have no room for you on our farm. But I guess you can stay out back in the barn.

[DONKEY, INNKEEPER, MARY, and JOSEPH take places in the stable stage right. The four ANGELS enter flapping their wings as if flying down the center aisle.]

ANGEL 1: I sang with all the angels who flew to earth to tell the shepherds of the Messiah's birth!

ANGEL 2: Jesus is born this day in tiny Bethlehem. A little town, but what a gem!

ANGEL 3: The littlest angels sang and tried not to squeak and through the stable's windows took a peek!

ANGEL 4: Angels here! Angels there! There were angels everywhere!

[ANGELS take their place at the back of the stable as SHEPHERDS enter down the aisle.]

SHEPHERD 1: *[carrying stuffed toy lamb]* I rejoiced the night my lost lamb was found. But when I saw the angels, I knew I was on holy ground.

SHEPHERD 2: My knees started shaking with sheer fright. *[shake knees]* When I saw all the angels in the sky that holy night!

SHEPHERD 3: We hurried to find where the babe did lay. He was sound asleep on a manger filled with hay.

SHEPHERD 4: My eyes were shut; I was sound asleep. The angels singing woke me and all my sheep!

[STAR enters down center aisle.]

STAR: I am the star that shone brilliantly. But there is a light, Who shines brighter than me. Baby Jesus is the light sent from God above. He is Heaven's gift to us filled with love.

[WISEMEN enter carrying gifts down center aisle.]

WISE MAN 1: *[kneel by manger and present gift]* The star in the sky was quite a sight. It was bumpy riding a camel all night!

WISE MAN 2: *[kneel by manger and present gift]* Gold I bring. To the newborn king!

WISE MAN 3: *[kneel by manger and present gift]* My gift is frankincense! It's for the tiny prince!

[The nativity scene should be set up at this point.]

ALL: To *you [point to audience]* a child is born!

Children sing "Away in a Manger."

[Blackout.]

Santa's Christmas Tree

by JOHN COSPER

Summary: An all-star cast of fairy-tale characters attend Santa's Christmas party for food, fellowship, and Santa's traditional telling of the birth of Christ.

Characters:
- Announcer—any age, gives story's introduction
- Santa—jolly, old elf who makes toys
- The Big Bad Wolf—hungry fairy-tale carnivore
- Cinderella, Sleeping Beauty, Snow White, Rapunzel—jilted fairy-tale princesses
- Little Bo Peep—a ditzy shepherd girl
- Rumpelstiltskin—a short guy who's a con artist
- Babe, Porky, and Hammy—The Three Pigs
- The Wicked Witch—Snow White's wicked stepmother
- Hansel and Gretel—candy-loving kids
- The Camel—a puppet who claims to be from a story
- Little Red Riding Hood, Goldilocks—cute little fairytale girls
- Bo Peep's Sheep—Sheep (nonspeaking roles)

Setting: the North Pole, elaborately decorated

Props: fairy-tale music, party favors, Christmas decorations, baby doll, a cross covered with a sheet, a stool, plate of cookies, glass of milk, buffet table with food, Christmas stockings (one with candy and one with coal)

Costumes: fairy tale costumes for all the characters; halo of tinsel for characters acting as angels; towels and headbands for Shepherds' headpieces for those acting as Shepherds, Mary, and Joseph

Lights out. Fairy-tale music plays to open scene.

Announcer: Once upon a time, in a faraway land of fairy tales, Santa hosted a Christmas party. Everyone came from miles around for this night of celebration to hear Santa tell the Christmas story and to witness the unveiling of the Christmas tree.

[Lights up. The stage is set for a party. A cross is standing at upstage center, covered by a sheet. The sheet should be set over the cross to make it look like a Christmas tree underneath. The CAMEL is sitting behind a table stage left with HANSEL and GRETEL. A buffet table is set up stage right, and BO PEEP'S SHEEP are gathered around it eating. RUMPELSTILTSKIN stands behind them, trying to get at the buffet. SNOW WHITE, the WITCH, and THE THREE PIGS are down stage right. BO PEEP is down stage left, pouting. The other characters mingle at center stage.]

BABE: Mmmm! This is delicious. Snow White, you gotta have some of this fruitcake!

SNOW: Fruitcake? Do you know how much fat is in that?

BABE: I don't care about fat grams! I'm a pig!

RUMPEL: *[yells]* Hey, Peep! Peep, your sheep are hogging the buffet! Come on, get 'em out of my way!

BABE: Just leave it to me! *["Baaa!" and move away from the buffet.]*

RUMPEL: Thanks, Babe.

BABE: Don't mention it.

[THE WICKED WITCH and THE BIG BAD WOLF walk to down stage left and take their place. The WOLF and the WITCH carry Christmas stockings.]

WOLF: Hey, Queenie!

WITCH: Hey, Big Bad. What did you get from Santa?

WOLF: Same as always. A stocking full of coal!

WITCH: Loser! I got candy!

WOLF: Candy? How? Did you go good?

WITCH: Goodness no, honey. I just switched stockings with Gretel!

WOLF: It's good to be bad!

[The WOLF and the WITCH step back to center stage so HANSEL and GRETEL are seen.]

CAMEL: Wowee. I can't believe this! You're really Hansel and Gretel! This is truly an honor.

GRETEL: So . . . which story are you in?

HANSEL: Yeah. I've never heard any stories about a camel.

CAMEL: Well, you know, I was in . . . that one.

HANSEL: Which one?

Skits and Plays for Children

CAMEL: You know. The one with the camel!

GRETEL: There are no fairy tales about camels!

CAMEL: Yes there are! I was in it!

[CINDERELLA, SNOW WHITE, RAPUNZEL, and SLEEPING BEAUTY walk to down stage left in front of HANSEL, GRETEL, and the CAMEL.]

SNOW: Forget Prince Charming, I know just the guy for you. He's a little short, but he's a very sweet guy.

BEAUTY: Are you trying to set me up with a dwarf? What could we possibly have in *[yawn]* common?

SNOW: More than you know!

BEAUTY: Yeah? What's his name?

SNOW: Sleepy.

CAMEL: I got it! The Musicians of Bremen!

GRETEL: There were no camels in The Musicians of Bremen.

CAMEL: How the Camel Got His Hump! That's got camel in the title!

GRETEL: Those stories don't count! What fairy tale were you in?

[SANTA enters.]

CAMEL: Hey look! It's Santa!

[ALL, except the CAMEL, run to surround SANTA.]

SANTA: Ho, ho, ho! Merry Christmas everyone!

ALL: Merry Christmas, Santa.

SANTA: Hey, can I ask a question, does this suit make me look fat?

[ALL laugh at SANTA's joke.]

RED: Santa, I wanna hear the Christmas story now!

ALL: Yeah! Now! We wanna hear it now! Please?

SANTA: I don't know. Santa's pretty tired. I don't know if I can tell it without—

[CINDERELLA runs up with cookies and a glass of milk.]

CINDY: Milk and cookies?
SANTA: That's my girl! Thank you, Cinderella!

[RUMPELSTILTSKIN sets a stool next to SANTA. SANTA puts the cookies and milk on the stool. He eats one cookie and drinks some milk. The rest of the cast sits on the stage behind SANTA in a semicircle. SANTA faces the audience as he begins.]

SANTA: Long ago, in a far away land, there lived a man named Joseph and a girl named Mary.

[SNOW WHITE and RUMPELSTILTSKIN stand up.]

SANTA: Mary and Joseph were engaged, but before they were married, Mary was visited by an angel who said . . .

[CINDERELLA stands up as the angel.]

CINDY: Do not be afraid, for you have found favor in the eyes of God. You will give birth to a son. He will be called the Son of the Most High, and His kingdom will never end.
SANTA: Soon after the angel appeared to Mary, the same angel appeared to Joseph.
CINDY: Joseph, do not be afraid to take Mary as your wife. The child that is inside of her is from the Holy Spirit, and you shall give Him the name Jesus.
SANTA: So Joseph took Mary as his wife, just like the angel told him. When the time came for the baby to be born, Joseph and Mary were in Joseph's hometown of Bethlehem. All the inns were full, so baby Jesus was born in a stable.

[RED RIDING HOOD hands SNOW WHITE a doll to be the baby. SNOW WHITE and RUMPELSTILTSKIN kneel down center stage with the baby.]

SANTA: He spent that first night lying in a manger, surrounded by pigs, sheep, and even a camel.

[THE THREE LITTLE PIGS and SHEEP gather around SNOW WHITE and RUMPELSTILTSKIN.]

CAMEL: See, I told you I was in this story!

SANTA: On that same night, a group of shepherds were watching their flocks.

[BO PEEP, RED RIDING HOOD, and GOLIDILOCKS (the Shepherds) stand up at stage left.]

SANTA: Suddenly, the angel of the Lord appeared to them, saying,

CINDY: Fear not, I bring you good news for all people. Today in the city of Bethlehem, a Savior has been born, who is Christ the Lord.

[SLEEPING BEAUTY, the WITCH, RAPUNZEL, and GRETEL [Angels] stand up with CINDERELLA.]

SANTA: Suddenly a host of angels appeared, singing praises to God. The shepherds ran into Bethlehem and found everything just as the angel had told them.

[The shepherds kneel around SNOW WHITE, RUMPELSTILTSKIN, and the animals. The angels begin singing "O Come All Ye Faithful" softly. The WOLF, the PRINCE, and HANSEL stand up and walk into the scene as the three Magi.]

SANTA: Some time later, Wise Men from the east visited the newborn king. They followed a star to Bethlehem, bringing Jesus gifts of gold and spices fit for a king.

[GRETEL and SLEEPING BEAUTY walk backstage to the cross, standing on either side of it.]

SANTA: But great as those gifts were, the greatest present given that night was the tiny baby in the manger. As a child he was only the son of a carpenter. As a man, He became known as the Son of God. That is why, on this cold December night, we remember the baby. We remember the angels who sang. We remember the gifts of the Wise Men. And if we are truly wise, we remember the gift this tiny baby would one day give on another tree, the greatest gift of all.

[GRETEL and SLEEPING BEAUTY rip off the sheet, revealing the cross. The angels sing the end of the verse, then lights out. Blackout.]

A Donkey's Story

by ALYCE PICKETT

Summary: In a rhythmic and poetic monologue, the donkey that Joseph and Mary rode into Bethlehem tells his side of the story of Christ's birth.
Character: DONKEY—male or female
Setting: outside the stable where Christ was born
Costume: donkey outfit

Lights up on DONKEY.

DONKEY: If I could talk, I'd tell you a story. Every word is true, even though it comes from me, Joseph's little brown donkey.

My master's wife rode one day on my back a long, long way. Up and down each rocky hill I plodded on the way until we reached the town of Bethlehem as day's light was growing dim.

I was as tired as could be and when he came again, we three went to a stable, nice and quiet and they stayed there with me that night. I got next to the wall and lay after eating my fill of hay.

Soon I slept . . . heard nothing more 'til shepherd men were at the door. From sheepfold they had come to bring praises to a Christ child king.

What is this? I stood to see in the manger a new baby. *Is that a King?* I wondered then, *Will He rule in the lives of men? How could I praise this baby King?* I couldn't shout, I couldn't sing.

I was very happy that He shared the stable there with me. I only want to let you know what happened that night long ago, and ask a favor now of you, Praise the Christ child for me too. *[Blackout.]*

The Christmas Toys

by JOHN COSPER

Summary: A story about two toys that want to know who is the greatest
Christmas gift of all.

Characters:

NARRATOR—lines could be said from offstage

CAPTAIN JOHNNY JUMPKICK—any age male, dressed as a little boy's
action figure

BONNIE BRIGHT-EYES—any age female, dressed as a little girl's doll

SANTA CLAUS

MARY

JOSEPH

Setting: *[by scene]*

Underneath a Christmas tree—wrapped presents, gifts propped up, large
tree trunk at center [if possible]

Bethlehem—manger scene

Props: Christmas tree; a big, red ball; wrapped Christmas packages; a
manger; baby doll for the baby Jesus

Costumes: space suit, little girl dress, Santa suit, Bible-times costumes

Director's Notes: The flow of the play has rhythmic pattern like a poem
so the exchanges between characters should flow as such to complete
the rhymes.

Scene 1: Underneath the Christmas Tree

*JOHNNY and BONNIE are on stage sleeping beside a big red ball. NARRATOR
should be off to the side of the stage [or offstage] for all of his lines.*

NARRATOR: Once upon a snowy eve, the Christmas lights were gleaming
From all around a Christmas tree to three small toys still sleeping.
A Captain Johnny Jumpkick toy slept by a big, red ball.
The third toy was the first awake—a Bonnie Bright-eyes doll.

BONNIE: It's Christmas Eve! Wake up! Wake up!

NARRATOR: She shouted with a grin.

JOHNNY: Aw knock it off,

NARRATOR: Johnny snapped back.

JOHNNY: I'm trying to sleep in.

BONNIE: The time has come. It's finally here! And soon one lucky girl
    Will wake and find me sitting here—the best gift in the world.

JOHNNY: I don't think so,

NARRATOR: Said Johnny Jumpkick hopping to his feet.

JOHNNY: No silly doll can do the things that make this hero neat!

BONNIE: I'm not,

NARRATOR: She huffed,

BONNIE: A silly doll, and if you're really bright,
    You'd see in every way that I'm a little girl's delight!
    I'm a limited edition and they call me Bonnie Bright-Eyes.
    I'm the only doll you'll ever see who blinks and winks and cries.
    The girls all love my pretty dress and hair that they can comb.
    The only thing I really need is somewhere to call home.

NARRATOR: She ended with a bow and followed with a graceful twirl.
    Then Johnny said,

JOHNNY: You've much to learn, you silly, silly girl!
    I'm Captain Johnny Jumpkick and as anyone can see,
    I'm easily a cooler toy than you will ever be!
    I use my ninja powers to fight green monsters from space
    And nobody has ever beat my spaceship in a race!

NARRATOR: The two stared at each other while the ball made not a peep,
    Because everybody knows a big, red ball cannot speak.
    Then Bonnie said,

BONNIE: We're wasting time by getting in a fight.
    There's only one way we can know which one of us is right.
    We have to go and ask the man whose beard grows white and thick.

NARRATOR: Then Johnny said,

JOHNNY: You're right! We'll have to ask dear old St. Nick!

NARRATOR: And even as he said that name, they heard a strange new sound
    As down the chimney Santa dropped and landed on the ground.

[SANTA enters.]

BONNIE and JOHNNY: Good, Santa!

NARRATOR: Cried the two small toys,

BONNIE: Please share with us your wisdom,

JOHNNY: And tell us who's the greatest gift throughout the Christmas
    kingdom!

NARRATOR: The jolly, fat man laughed as only Santa Claus can do,
    And said,

SANTA: I think I know just how to help the two of you.
    We'll have to take a journey to a land that's far away
    To show you why we celebrate with gifts on Christmas Day.
    We're going back in time, where the two of you will see
    A gift that came one Christmas Day that changed all history.

Scene 2: Bethlehem

The toys exit with SANTA. *As the* NARRATOR *speaks,* MARY *and* JOSEPH *enter
with the baby Jesus and walk to the side of stage that is decorated like
Bethlehem.* JOHNNY, BONNIE, *and* SANTA *then reenter.*

NARRATOR: The toys agreed and with a wink were quickly swept away
    And found themselves flying away in Santa's reindeer sleigh.
    They traveled far into the night 'til both were half asleep,
    Then softly were awakened by the gentle baa of sheep.
    The sleigh had landed in a barn of animals and hay
    And a couple near a manger where a tiny baby lay.
    Bonnie looked and Johnny looked to find the special toy,
    The greatest gift that anyone could give a girl or boy.
    But everywhere the toys would look, no packages were found,
    So Bonnie asked St. Nick,

BONNIE: Where can this greatest gift be found?

JOHNNY: What is it, Santa?

NARRATOR: Johnny asked,

JOHNNY: A teddy bear or ball?
    Where is this special toy you call the greatest gift of all?

SANTA: The greatest gift,

NARRATOR: Santa began,

SANTA: Is not a ball or doll,
    In fact the Christmas present here is not a toy at all!
    Look at the child who's sleeping softly in His mother's arms,
    The child who's snuggled tightly in old rags to keep Him warm.
    Look in the eyes of that small child and surely you will find

It's Jesus Christ, the King of kings and Savior of mankind!

NARRATOR: Bonnie was shocked.

BONNIE: This can't be right, this baby that we've found,

How can a baby be the greatest gift of all?

NARRATOR: She frowned.

Then Santa smiled and said,

SANTA: This gift is more than just a toy.

It's God the Father's perfect gift of love and peace and joy.

God sent His only Son to earth to die upon a cross.

He came to set His people free and save a world that's lost.

He came to give the world new life by giving His away,

And that's the very reason we give gifts on Christmas Day.

NARRATOR: Then Captain Johnny Jumpkick and the Bonnie
Bright-Eyes doll

Approached the newborn King sleeping in the stable stall.

They kneeled with Santa by the child amid the hay and grass

And there inside the stable found the greatest gift at last!

[Blackout.]

Four Questions of Christmas

by PHYLLIS WEZEMAN

Summary: A Christmas parallel to the Passover dinner in which four children ask questions about the significance of Jesus' birth.

Characters:

NARRATOR

FOUR CHILDREN

Setting: home that is being decorated on Christmas Eve

Props: decorated Christmas tree, extra ornaments to be put on tree, nativity scene, wrapped presents, bows to put on presents, stool for NARRATOR

Running Time: 5 minutes

[The NARRATOR sits on a stool off to one side with a separate spotlight. The FOUR CHILDREN are gathered around the tree. They can be placing ornaments on the tree, putting bows on presents and arranging them beneath the tree, or setting up the nativity scene.]

NARRATOR: Often traditions become so ingrained that families go through the motions of the holidays without stopping to think about the reasons behind seasonal celebrations. The Jewish religion understood the need to encourage examination of customs and traditions. The celebration of Passover, for example, would not be complete without the asking of the "four questions" that require the older generation to explain the reasons behind the ritual of the Seder meal to the youngest people present. Since Christmas is the celebration of the arrival of a baby to His Jewish parents, perhaps it would be appropriate to adopt this Jewish custom of asking questions in order to celebrate His birth.

CHILD ONE: On other days we go to church in the morning. Why on this night do we go to church so late?

NARRATOR: On Christmas Eve we remember that it was at night as the shepherds watched their sheep that the angels came to announce the birth of a special baby. The shepherds heard the angel chorus because they were awake and watching. On Christmas Eve we want to be awake and watching for the birth of Jesus too. So we share a special service with our friends at church to remember that Jesus, the Prince of Peace, was born in the gentle quiet of the night.

CHILD TWO: When it is someone's birthday, we usually take presents to the birthday girl or boy. Why on Jesus' birthday do we give presents to one another?

NARRATOR: On Jesus' birthday we give presents because the wise men took gifts of gold, frankincense, and myrrh to the baby Jesus. Jesus also taught us that the way to show our love for Him is to love one another. So on Christmas we share gifts, as the wise men did, but we share them with others in Jesus' name.

CHILD THREE: For no other holiday do we put up a tree inside the house. Why for this holiday do we bring a tree inside and put lights on it?

NARRATOR: Many years ago in Germany, the tradition of using a lighted tree at Christmas was begun. The green boughs of the evergreen tree symbolize for us that the gift Jesus brings is eternal life. The twinkling lights remind us that Jesus is the light of the world. The beauty of the lighted Christmas tree suggests the beauty of God's love for the world, a love that sent Jesus, God's only Son.

CHILD FOUR: At no other time do we set up a nativity scene. Why only at Christmas do we worship the baby in the manger?

NARRATOR: We worship God Almighty, the maker of the universe. Yet our human bodies cannot see or understand the power that God is. Because God wanted us to know how much we are loved, Jesus came as a baby, a human, just like us. The nativity scene reminds us of how God's love came to earth, love made known in Jesus, our Savior.

[Lights dim. All bow their heads as "Away in a Manger" or another appropriate Christmas song is sung.]

C-H-R-I-S-T-M-A-S Is . . .

by MARY TUCKER

Summary: A presentation about Jesus' birth, using the letters in the word *Christmas.*

Characters:

Nine Letter Holders

Children's Chorus (to sing Christmas carols)

Three Verse Reciters

Three Actors

Props: nine large letter cards spelling *Christmas;* a large, gift-wrapped package (the top wrapped separately so it can be easily lifted off) with a word card inside that says, "Eternal Life"; a sign that says, "Tell everyone that Jesus is the Reason for the Season!"

Running Time: 15 minutes

Program Notes: If you have a limited number of children, you do not need a separate children's chorus. One child can play the parts of all three Actors. One child can read all the Bible verses.

For younger children, have children hold up each letter of *Christmas* as an older narrator reads each rhyme.

Letter Holder One *[holds up letter C]:* Christmas is **carols** that we sing with joy, celebrating the birthday of God's little boy.

C H R

[CHILDREN'S CHORUS sings "Joy to the World."]

LETTER HOLDER TWO *[holds up letter H]:* Christmas is **hope** for the whole human race. Our hope is in Jesus who died in our place.

VERSE RECITER ONE: "We have put our hope in the living God, who is the Savior of all men, and especially of those who believe" (1 Timothy 4:10).

LETTER HOLDER THREE *[holds up letter R]:* Christmas is **receiving** the gift God gives—Jesus His Son—so that we may live.

ACTOR ONE *[holds up a gift-wrapped package and pretends to read label]:* From GOD *[points upward]* to YOU! *[points to audience; then opens package and removes card that says ETERNAL LIFE, holding it up for all to see]*

LETTER HOLDER FOUR *[holds up letter I]:* Christmas is **Immanuel**—the Son's special name that says God is with us! That's why He came.

[CHILDREN'S CHORUS sings "O Come, All Ye Faithful."]

LETTER HOLDER FIVE *[holds up letter S]:* Christmas is **shepherds** leaving their sheep to go see God's Son in a manger asleep.

VERSE RECITER TWO: "The shepherds returned, glorifying and praising God for all the things they had heard and seen" (Luke 2:20).

LETTER HOLDER SIX *[holds up letter T]:* Christmas is **telling** people we know that Jesus the Savior was born long ago.

[ACTOR TWO holds up a sign that says, "Tell everyone that Jesus is the Reason for the Season!"]

LETTER HOLDER SEVEN *[holds up letter M]:* Christmas is a **manger** in a poor cattle stall. The baby who slept there is Lord of us all.

[CHILDREN'S CHORUS sings "Away in a Manger."]

LETTER HOLDER EIGHT *[holds up letter A]:* Christmas is **angels** filling the sky, praising the Lord on earth and on high.

ACTOR THREE *[waves arms overhead and shouts]:* Glory to God in the highest and on earth!

LETTER HOLDER NINE *[holds up letter S]:* Christmas is **special,** don't you agree? For Jesus, God's Son, came for you and for me!

VERSE RECITER THREE: "For God so loved the world that he gave his one and only Son, that whoever believes in him shall not perish but have eternal life" (John 3:16).

[CHILDREN'S CHORUS sings "Hark, The Herald Angels Sing."]

M A S

The Story of the Wise Men

by PHYLLIS WEZEMAN

Summary: A dramatic retelling of the story of the Magi.

Characters:
- Narrator
- Wise Man One
- Wise Man Two
- Wise Man Three
- Herod
- Priests (2 or more children)
- Chief Priest

Setting: home that is being decorated on Christmas Eve

Props: copies of the script (optional props—see program notes)

Running Time: 10 minutes

Program Notes

This program is designed to be flexible both in presentation and in the number of children involved. Presentation will vary based on skills, preparation time, and performance needs. In Sunday school classes or worship services, a simple choral reading may be done with stools for actors and music stands to hold scripts, or readers may be scattered throughout the congregation and speak from the pews. A more elaborate production with costumes and memorized parts would make a meaningful seasonal program or devotion. Props needed for a dramatic production include Bible costumes for Herod, kings, and priests; a large, decorated throne for Herod; wise men's gifts; a doll for the child Jesus; and a child to play the non-speaking character of Mary.

To involve more children, create larger acting groups to represent the wise men and priests.

No matter the level of presentation, participants should be encouraged to practice the script aloud several times and to rehearse when to stand and speak. Readers should be reminded to breathe deeply and project voices, to read with feeling, slowly and distinctly.

Narrator *[facing congregation]:* Now when Jesus was born in Bethlehem of Judea in the days of Herod the King *[Herod stands, smiles, and* *gestures in a kingly way],* behold, wise men from the east came to Jerusalem *[three WISE MEN stand]* saying,

WISE MAN ONE: Where is He who has been born king of the Jews?

WISE MAN TWO: For we have seen His star in the east,

WISE MAN THREE: And have come to worship Him. *[All bow from the waist.]*

NARRATOR: When Herod the king heard this, he was troubled *[HEROD stands, growls, and complains]* and all Jerusalem with him. *[PRIESTS growl and complain.]* And assembling all the chief priests and scribes of the people *[PRIESTS stand],* he inquired of them:

HEROD: Where is the Christ supposed to be born?

PRIESTS: In Bethlehem of Judea, for so it is written by the prophet:

CHIEF PRIEST: And you, O Bethlehem, in the land of Judah, are by no means least among the rulers of Judah; for from you shall come a ruler who will govern my people Israel.

NARRATOR: Then Herod summoned the wise men secretly and ascertained from them what time the star appeared. *[HEROD gestures and WISE MEN turn toward HEROD.]* And he sent them to Bethlehem, saying:

HEROD *[insincerely]:* Go and search diligently for the child, and when you have found him, bring me word, that I too may come and worship him. *[WISE MEN bow and nod agreement.]*

NARRATOR: When they had heard the king, they went their way. *[HEROD and PRIESTS sit.]*

WISE MEN: Let's go! Follow that star! There it goes!

NARRATOR: And lo, the star which they had seen in the east went before them, till it came to rest over the place where the child was.

WISE MAN ONE: In that stable?

NARRATOR: When they saw the star, they rejoiced exceedingly!

WISE MEN *[quietly]:* Yay!

NARRATOR: And going into the house, they saw the child with Mary his mother, and they fell down and worshiped him. *[WISE MEN bow, or kneel, and look worshipful.]* Then, opening their treasures, they offered Him gifts.

WISE MAN ONE: Gold!

WISE MAN TWO: Frankincense!

WISE MAN THREE: And myrrh!

NARRATOR: And being warned in a dream not to return to Herod *[WISE MEN make a "sh-h-h-h!" sign and pretend to tiptoe away as HEROD stands],* they departed to their own country by another way. *[WISE MEN sit as HEROD looks around, and then shrugs and sits.]*

NARRATOR: And so ends our lesson of the visit of the wise men. Let those who are wise still listen to the angels' voices and follow the light of the Bethlehem star! *[NARRATOR sits.]*

The First Christmas

by ALYCE PICKETT

Summary: A short retelling of the Christmas story using rhyme.

Characters:

JOSEPH

MARY

ANGELS

SHEPHERDS

MAGI

STAR

NARRATOR

CHILDREN'S CHOIR

Props: large, printed name cards on string to go around the neck of each character; costumes for characters, such as angels' robes, shepherds' staffs, a glittery poster board star (all optional)

[The characters may line up in groups in order. Each group may step forward when it is their turn to speak.]

JOSEPH: Mary and I came a long, long way
                And reached Bethlehem late one day;
                So late we could find no room at all.
                We rested that night in a cattle stall.

MARY: That night I welcomed my baby son,
                Little Lord Jesus, the holy one.
                For God had chosen me to be
                The mother of the Christ-baby.

[CHILDREN'S CHOIR sings "O Little Town of Bethlehem."]

ANGELS: That night God sent us down to earth
                With the good news of Jesus' birth.
                Rejoicing, we sang praises, and then

We went back to Heaven again.

SHEPHERDS: Outside Bethlehem that dark night
We saw heavenly angels bright
And heard the news they came to
    bring
About the little Christ-child king.

[CHILDREN'S CHOIR sings "Silent Night."]

MAGI: We saw the new star appear
And knew God's promised one was
    here.
We traveled far our gifts to bring
To this little Christ-child king.

STAR: The Magi rested every day;
Then I helped them find their way.
High in the sky, shining bright,
I guided them throughout the night.

[CHILDREN'S CHOIR sings "We Three Kings of Orient Are."]

NARRATOR: Remember now that wonderful night.
Worship again the Lord of light.
Together now our praises bring
To Lord and Savior, risen king!

[CHILDREN'S CHOIR sings "Joy to the World."]

A Christmas to Remember

Summary: A simple acting out of the Christmas story with a backdrop of Scripture for preschool and young elementary children.

Characters:
- NARRATOR
- ANGELS
- MARY
- JOSEPH
- DECREE HOLDER
- DONKEY
- SHEPHERDS
- SHEEP
- STAR HOLDER
- WISE MEN

Props: Bible costumes for MARY and JOSEPH; a manger with hay; a doll for baby Jesus; ears for SHEEP and the DONKEY; white robes for ANGELS; a scroll-like, official-looking paper for Caesar's decree; a recorded sound of a donkey's *hee haw* (if possible); staffs for SHEPHERDS; a glittery star attached to a dowel or ruler to hold high in the air; an older-looking doll for toddler Jesus; gifts for WISE MEN; two large painted poster board backdrops—a desert with a palm tree and a stable (optional)

Running Time: 10-15 minutes

Program Notes: This program can be done with almost any number of children and is very simple to organize and practice. There are no actual speaking parts for children to memorize, only actions. Older children can be assigned the parts of MARY, JOSEPH, and the WISE MEN. The NARRATOR should be an adult, and you will need several adults sitting in front to cue children at the appropriate times.

[The desert backdrop should be set up stage left and the stable backdrop with the manger in front of it stage right. The children may stand in groups in the center of the stage. An ANGEL and MARY should be stage left.]

Narrator: Over 2,000 years ago, God sent the angel Gabriel to Nazareth, a town in Galilee, to a woman named Mary who was pledged to be married to a man named Joseph. *[Mary kneels before the Angel in fear. The Angel places his hand on Mary's shoulder to comfort her.]* The angel said, "Do not be afraid, Mary. You have found favor with God. You will be with child and give birth to a Son, and you are to give Him the name Jesus."

[Mary nods her head up and down in agreement.] "I am the Lord's servant," Mary answered. "May it be to me as you have said." Then the angel left her. *[The Angel leaves.]*

[Joseph joins Mary on the stage left.]

Narrator: In those days, Caesar Augustus issued a decree that a census should be taken of the entire Roman world. *[Decree Holder walks across stage in front of Joseph and Mary holding his decree in front of him and pretending to read loudly from it.]*
Joseph also went up from the town of Nazareth in Galilee to Bethlehem, the town of David, because he belonged to the house and line of David. *[Donkey moves in a* hee haw *motion across stage as prompted by recorded* hee haw *sounds. Joseph and Mary follow Donkey across stage.]* He went there to register with Mary, who was pledged to be married to him and was expecting a child. *[Joseph puts his arm around Mary and smiles widely.]* But there was no room for them in the Bethlehem inn, so they stayed in a stable. *[Joseph and Mary shrug and settle in on either side of manger.]* While they were there, the time came for Mary's baby to be born. She had her firstborn, a Son, and she wrapped Him in cloths and laid Him in a manger. *[Adult hands Mary baby Jesus and she cuddles Him and lays Him in the manger.]*

[Shepherds move to stage left.]

Narrator: And there were shepherds living out in the fields nearby, keeping watch over their flocks at night. *[Sheep baa several times.]* An angel of the Lord appeared to them, and they were terrified. *[Angel moves to stage left and pretends to speak to Shepherds as they fall to the ground in fear.]* But the angel said, "Do not be afraid. I bring you good news of great joy that will be for all the people. Today in the town of David a Savior has been born to you; He is Christ the Lord. This will be a sign to you: You will find a baby wrapped in clothes and lying in a manger."

Suddenly a great company of the heavenly host appeared with the angel, praising God and saying *[other ANGELS turn and face SHEPHERDS and wave arms and pretend to sing]*, "Glory to God in the highest, and on earth peace to men on whom His favor rests."

[ANGELS leave. SHEPHERDS get up and look at each other and gesture excitedly. SHEEP baa.]

NARRATOR: When the angels had left them and gone into Heaven, the shepherds said to one another, "Let's go to Bethlehem and see this thing that has happened, which the Lord has told us about." *[SHEPHERDS walk across stage and bow in front of manger.]* So they hurried off and found Mary and Joseph, and the baby, who was lying in the manger.

[SHEPHERDS return to center group. WISE MEN move stage left.

Stage right, remove manger and set up a chair for MARY *to sit in with* JOSEPH *behind her, an older doll in her lap.]*

NARRATOR: After Jesus was born in Bethlehem in Judea, during the time of King Herod, Wise Men from the east saw a star in the east. They knew that a king had been born and came to worship Him. *[STAR HOLDER holds up star in air, and* WISE MEN *follow it across the stage to where Jesus is.]* On coming to the house, they saw the child with His mother, Mary, and they bowed down and worshiped Him. *[WISE MEN bow before Jesus and present their gifts one at a time, as the narrator says them.]* Then they presented Him with gifts of gold and of incense and of myrrh.

[MARY, JOSEPH, and WISE MEN, *rise and move to center stage.]*

NARRATOR: *[Each group bows their head when the narrator mentions them. The* DECREE *and* STAR HOLDER *may bow their heads with the* WISE MEN.*]* And so Mary and Joseph, the angels, the shepherds with their sheep, and the wise men all worshiped and welcomed Jesus, God's only Son.

Christmas Celebration of Love

by CAROLYN R. SCHEIDIES

Summary: A choral and dramatic program for preschool through 6th grade.

Characters:
  NARRATOR 1
  NARRATOR 2
  MARY, JOSEPH, SHEPHERDS (non-speaking parts)
  GRADES 5 AND 6
  GRADES 1 AND 2
  GRADES 3 AND 4
  PRESCHOOL

Props: baby doll; manger; cross in background; Bible costumes for MARY, JOSEPH, SHEPHERDS; decorated Christmas tree; tinsel; wrapped gifts

Running Time: 45 minutes

Program Notes: This program can be adapted to almost any number of children. Songs are suggestions only. Substitute your children's favorite Christmas songs about Jesus.

When the program refers to ALL singing, the congregation may join in with the children.

[GRADES 1–6 are lined up on stage left. NARRATORS are stage right in front of a Christmas tree with lights and presents. The manger scene is in the center of the stage. A spotlight focuses on NARRATOR 1 as he begins to speak.]

NARRATOR 1: "But you, Bethlehem Ephrathah, though you are small among the clans of Judah, out of you will come for me one who will be ruler over Israel, whose origins are from of old, from ancient times" (Micah 5:2).

[ALL sing "Joy to the World."]

NARRATOR 1: "In those days Caesar Augustus issued a decree that a census should be taken of the entire Roman world. (This was the first census that took place while Quirinius was governor of Syria.) And everyone went to his own town to register. So Joseph also went up from the town of Nazareth in Galilee to Judea, to Bethlehem the town of David, because he belonged to the house and line of David" (Luke 2:1-4).

NARRATOR 2: "He went there to register with Mary, who was pledged to be married to him and was expecting a child. While they were there, the time came for the baby to be born, and she gave birth to her firstborn, a son. She wrapped him in cloths and placed him in a manger, because there was no room for them in the inn" (Luke 2:5-7).

[ALL sing "O Little Town of Bethlehem." As they sing, MARY and JOSEPH come down the aisle and onto center stage where MARY kneels by the manger as JOSEPH stands beside her.]

GRADES 5 AND 6: Christmas comes but once a year,

GRADES 1 AND 2: A time of joy and celebration.

GRADES 3 AND 4: But Jesus didn't come to make a splash,

ALL: He came to bring humankind salvation.

[ALL sing "O Come, All Ye Faithful" as PRESCHOOL lines up on stage.]

PRESCHOOL: I may be small,
    But this I know is true,
    Jesus came to earth because
    He loves me *[point to self]* and you *[point to audience].*

[ALL sing "O Come, Let Us Adore Him" as PRESCHOOL returns to sit with their parents.]

NARRATOR 1: "And there were shepherds living out in the fields nearby, keeping watch over their flocks at night. An angel of the Lord appeared to them, and the glory of the Lord shone around them, and they were terrified" (Luke 2:8, 9).

NARRATOR 2: "But the angel said to them, 'Do not be afraid. I bring you good news of great joy that will be for all the people. Today in the town of David a Savior has been born to you; he is Christ the Lord. This will be a sign to you: You will find a baby wrapped in cloths and lying in a manger'" (Luke 2:10-12).

[ALL sing verse one of "Away in a Manger" as GRADES 1 AND 2 line up in three groups on either side and behind manger.]

GROUP 1: The manger is but the start of a journey *[motion toward manger]*,

GROUP 2: That continued to the cross *[motion toward cross behind manger]*

GROUP 3: Where Jesus sacrificed His life *[arms crossed on chest, heads bowed]*

ALL GRADES 1 AND 2: But, oh, how great the cost.

[ALL sing verse two of "Away in a Manger" as GRADES 1 AND 2 return to choral group.]

NARRATOR 2: "Suddenly a great company of the heavenly host appeared with the angel, praising God and saying, 'Glory to God in the highest, and on earth peace to men on whom his favor rests'" (Luke 2:13, 14).

[ALL sing "Angels from the Realms of Glory" while SHEPHERDS come down the aisle, go up on stage, and kneel in front of the manger. GRADES 3 AND 4 move to the front of the group.]

GRADES 3 AND 4: He didn't leave His glory

SOLO CHILD: For tinsel, gifts, and trees. *[If church is decorated with a tree, indicate it.]*

SOLO CHILD: He came to offer forgiveness and hope *[hand over heart]*,

GRADES 3 AND 4: And to set His people free *[arms out]*.

NARRATOR 2: "The Spirit of the Sovereign LORD is on me, because the LORD has anointed me to preach good news to the poor. He has sent me to bind up the brokenhearted, to proclaim freedom for the captives and release from darkness for the prisoners" (Isaiah 61:1).

GRADES 3 AND 4: Dying on the cross He showed

SOLO CHILD: A love so great and true. *[form heart in the air]*

SOLO CHILD: He died and yet He rose again, *[raise hands, palm up, from knees to above shoulders]*

GRADES 3 AND 4: All for me and you. *[indicate self, audience]*

[ALL sing "Hark! The Herald Angels Sing" while GRADES 3 AND 4 return to their places. GRADES 5 AND 6 move forward and make two semicircles on either side of the manger scene.]

NARRATOR 1: "The LORD has done great things for us, and we are filled with joy" (Psalm 126:3).

SEMICIRCLE 1: In the business of the season,

SEMICIRCLE 2: Let us not forget the one

SEMICIRCLE 1: Whose birthday that we celebrate

GRADES 5 AND 6: God's one and only Son.

NARRATOR 1: "The people walking in darkness have seen a great light; on those living in the land of the shadow of death a light has dawned" (Isaiah 9:2).

NARRATOR 2: "For God did not send his Son into the world to condemn the world, but to save the world through him" (John 3:17).

[ALL sing "God Sent His Son" to the tune "God Is So Good."]

SEMICIRCLE 1: Let us not forget the cross *[spotlight on cross in* *background]* shadows the manger scene *[spotlight on manger],*

SEMICIRCLE 2: For the gift He gave was the gift of life He offers you and me.

NARRATOR 2: "For God so loved the world that he gave his one and only Son, that whoever believes in him shall not perish but have eternal life" (John 3:16).

NARRATOR 1: Christmas comes but once a year *[kneels before manger],*

NARRATOR 2: Oh, what a celebration *[kneels before manger].*

ALL CHILDREN: As today we bow before our Lord *[bow heads and face manger]*

ALL: To accept His great salvation.

[ALL sing "Joy to the World."]

Presents

by ANNA M. CAISON

A Christmas skit for primary children.

ALL: Jesus gives us presents all year round.

CHILD 1: He gave me a mommy and a daddy to show me His love. *(Unwraps a picture of parents.)*

CHILD 2: He gave me His Word so I can read about Him. *(Unwraps a Bible.)*

CHILD 3: He gave me a new family! A spiritual family to help me grow up in Him. *(Unwraps a picture of church members.)*

CHILD 4: He sends His Holy Spirit to help me when trouble comes my way. *(Unwraps a drawing of a dove with the caption: Holy Spirit.)*

CHILD 5: He called me to be His very own. And if I love and follow Him, He'll take me one day to live with Him. *(Unwraps a drawing of the kingdom of God with an inset of child's picture.)*

CHILD 6: He gave us himself so we can live forever with Him. *(Unwraps the word JESUS on a large poster.)*

ALL: Thank You, Jesus, for giving us presents all year round.

The Best Gift

by CAROLYN R. SCHIEDIES

For six individuals or groups. Groups 1-3 face 4-6.

SONG: "Angels, from the Realms of Glory" *(first verse only)*

1:   *(Thumbing though book):* It's Christmastime.
    I want a toy;
    I want a book
    With lots of pictures to enjoy.

SONG: "Jingle Bells" *(one verse)*

2:   *(Pretending to drive a play truck):* I want a truck
    That goes vrr-oom
    And enough presents
    To fill a whole room. *(arms outstretched)*

SONG: "The Twelve Days of Christmas" *(five days)*

3:   *(Standing on tiptoes, indicate tall tree):* A big tall tree
    Would be great
    With lots of lights,
    And I could stay up very late. *(Hands on hips, nod.)*

SONG: "O Christmas Tree" *(one verse)*

4:   These things sound nice
    But don't you know *(shaking finger)*
    Christmas is more than gifts
    And trees that glow?

SONG: "O Little Town of Bethlehem" *(verse one)*

5: Christmas is Jesus
Coming from Heaven to earth, *(motion from Heaven to earth)*
Bringing us the best gift
Just by His birth. *(hold arms as though cuddling baby)*

Song: "O Little Town of Bethlehem" *(verse two)*

6: You see, He came
To live and die for you and me *(arms out)*
And conquer death
To make us free. *(raise arms in joy)*

Song: "O Little Town of Bethlehem" *(verse three)*

4 and 5:	He wants to give us more
1:	Than toys and trees.
6:	He offers help and hope and peace
2 and 3:	For all eternity.

Song: "O Little Town of Bethlehem" *(verse four)*

1 and 2:	It's OK to like presents *(Pretending to unwrap gift.)*
3 and 4:	But better yet to know
5 and 6:	And accept the greatest Gift *(Pointing up.)*
All:	Jesus Christ who loves us so. *(Hand over heart.)*
	"I have come that they may have life, and have it to the full"
	(John 10:10, *NIV*).

Song: "O Come, All Ye Faithful" *(verse one:1-3, verse two: 4-6, verse three and refrains: All)*

S-A-M-T-S-I-R-H-C Y-R-R-E-M

by DIXIE PHILLIPS

Fourteen children enter carrying poster boards on which letters have been written. All children hold their letters to their sides until the end when they show the letters for the congregation to read.

UNISON: We have a little letter game we'd like to play with you.
Let the fun begin with a few important clues.

[Child holding the poster board with the letter S and star on it says:]
S is for the star that shone that holy night.
I'm sure that it was glowing very, very bright.

[Child in a donkey costume says:]
A is for the animals that were in the stall.
I'm sure there must have been a donkey saying, *"Hee-haw!"*

[Girl dressed as Mary says:]
M is for Mary. She loved her tiny Son.
An angel had told her she was God's chosen one.

[Child carrying a stop sign says:]
T is for the traffic that showed up that holy night.
Many stopped to worship Him. It was quite a sight.

[Child dressed as a shepherd says:]
S is for the shepherds who left their flock of sheep
so they could bow before Him and worship at His feet.

[Child with sign which reads "I = ME" says:]
I is simply for little old me.
I'm the one He loves for all eternity.

[Child dressed as an angel says:]
R is for rejoicing. That's what the angels did.
It sounded heavenly and quite splendid.

[Child sits on a bale of hay and says:]
H is for the hay that filled the lowly manger.
The tiny King who lay there would be a life-changer.

[Child dressed like a mouse says:]
C is for the critters that were hiding in the stall.
I'm sure there was a mouse—the tiniest critter of all.

[Child points at congregation and then at self and says:]
Y is for you and you and you and you!
Unto you a Savior's born, and unto me too!

[Child dressed like an angel points at congregation and says:]
R is for the reason why our Savior came to earth.
You're the reason why angels sang of His birth.

[Child dressed as a wise man says:]
R is for the rich gifts that the wise men brought,
to the tiny baby whom for days they had sought.

[Child waves at congregation and says:]
E is for everyone Jesus came to save.
If you belong to Him, let me see you wave.

[Child holding the "M" sign says:]
M is for the many who believe upon God's Son.
He didn't come for some. He came for *everyone*.

UNISON: The time has come to solve our Christmas mystery.
We hope you weren't too confused by the letters you did see.
And what's the Christmas message for each one today?
Merry Christmas to all! Thanks for coming to our play.

Christmas Joy

by CAROLYN R. SCHIEDIES

Parts: Preschoolers, Chorus (Primaries, Middlers, and Preteens; each group has three sections), Narrators 1 and 2—contemporary dress, Mary, Joseph, and Shepherds—biblical dress
Props: Costumes, shepherds' staffs, manger, doll, cross
Scene: Empty manger, front center stage

Scriptures are from the *New International Version* of the Bible.

ENTRANCE: "Hark! the Herald Angels Sing" *(all come on stage singing first two verses)*

PRESCHOOLERS *(sit with parents after their recitation):*
We may be young and short and small, *(Hand on head)*
You all may be big and, oh, so tall; *(Raise hand indicating way tall)*
But we are big enough to say *(Stand proud, feet apart)*
Thank You, Jesus, for coming Christmas day. *(Fold hands and look up)*

NARRATOR 1: "The people walking in darkness have seen a great light; on those living in the land of the shadow of death a light has dawned" (Isaiah 9:2).
NARRATOR 2: "In the beginning was the Word, and the Word was with God, and the Word was God" (John 1:1).

(PRIMARIES, step to center stage in semicircle around manger.)

1: Jesus left His home,
2: Left a wonderful heavenly throne,
3: To come to us right here on earth
ALL: Came as a baby with a manger birth.

SONG: "Thou Didst Leave Thy Throne" *(stanza 1, "Thou didst leave thy throne . . .": PRIMARIES on the stanza, all on refrain. After song,*

PRIMARIES step back into CHORUS; MARY and JOSEPH slowly walk up aisle and kneel on either side of manger. Discreetly add doll.)

NARRATOR 1: "For to us a child is born, to us a son in given, and the government will be on his shoulders. And he will be called Wonderful Counselor, Mighty God, Everlasting Father, Prince of Peace. Of the increase of his government and peace there will be no end. He will reign on David's throne and over his kingdom, establishing and upholding it with justice and righteousness from that time on and forever. The zeal of the Lord Almighty will accomplish this" (Isaiah 9:6, 7).

NARRATOR 2: "While they were there, the time came for the baby to be born, and she gave birth to her firstborn, a son. She wrapped him in cloths and placed him in a manger, because there was no room for them in the inn" (Luke 2:6, 7).

(MIDDLERS step to center stage in semicircle around manger.)

1: We may be young, but we know the truth:
ALL: Jesus came for me and you.
2: Came to be both Savior and Lord,
3: Came as promised in His Word.

Skits and Plays for Children

Song: "Thou Didst Leave Thy Throne" *(stanza 2, "Heaven's arches rang . . .": Middlers on the stanza, all on refrain. After song, Middlers step back into chorus; Shepherds make their way down aisle and kneel before the manger.)*

Narrator 1: "All this took place to fulfill what the Lord had said through the prophet: 'The virgin will be with child and will give birth to a son, and they will call him Immanuel'—which means, 'God with us'" (Matthew 1:22, 23).

Narrator 2: "'Today in the town of David a Savior has been born to you; he is Christ the Lord. This will be a sign to you: You will find a baby wrapped in cloths and lying in a manger.'

"Suddenly a great company of the heavenly host appeared with the angel, praising God and saying, 'Glory to God in the highest, and on earth peace to men on whom his favor rests.' When the angels had left them and gone into heaven, the shepherds said to one another, 'Let's go to Bethlehem and see this thing that has happened, which the Lord has told us about.'

"So they hurried off and found Mary and Joseph, and the baby, who was lying in the manger. When they had seen him, they spread the word concerning what had been told them about this child" (Luke 2:11-17).

(Preteens step to center stage in semicircle around manger.)

1: Jesus came to bring both hope and life,
1 and 2: To take us to Him when we die.
  Solo: Big or small, what's important to know
    All: Is Jesus came because He loved us so.

Song: "Thou Didst Leave Thy Throne" *(stanza 4, "Thou Camest, O Lord . . .": Preteens on stanza, all on refrain. After song, Preteens step back into chorus; cross is highlighted behind chorus.)*

Narrator 1: "This is how God showed his love among us: He sent his one and only Son into the world that we might live through him. This is love: not that we loved God, but that he loved us and sent his Son as an atoning sacrifice for our sins" (1 John 4:9, 10).

NARRATOR 2: "But God demonstrates his own love for us in this: While we were still sinners, Christ died for us" (Romans 5:8).

PRETEENS: So we celebrate this day;

MIDDLERS: We make it special in every way

PRIMARIES: By laying aside our candy and toys

ALL: To worship our Savior with quiet Christmas joy.

(All kneel around manger.)

NARRATOR 1: "In him was life, and that life was the light of men" (John 1:4).

NARRATOR 2: "For the wages of sin is death, but the gift of God is eternal life in Christ Jesus our Lord" (Romans 6:23).

SONG: "Thou Didst Leave Thy Throne" *(stanza 5, "When the heavens . . .": solo on stanza, all on refrain.)*

(Optional: Director may chose to have thank yous and recognitions and/ or a closing prayer by the minister or other leader)

SONG: "Hark! the Herald Angels Sing" *(last stanza; all stand and designated student invites audience to join in singing).*

The Most Wonderful Christmas

by LILLIAN ROBBINS

Characters: *(Some characters without speaking parts)*

TED	JONAH'S MOM
MOM (Mrs. Tetterton)	JONAH'S DAD
DAD (Mr. Tetterton)	JONAH'S 2 BROTHERS and 1 SISTER
DANA (sister)	AUNT CHRISTY
GRANNY	CHRISTINA
POP	JIMMY
JONAH	BUTCH

Scene 1: Tetterton house before Christmas

Scene 2: Tetterton house on Christmas Day

Props: Centerpiece, tree, table (dining and small), chairs, stools (floor pillows or other sitting arrangements), dishes (one casserole containing food), presents

Scene 1

Mom is decorating the tree; TED rushes in very excited.

TED: Mom, I want to invite friends over for Christmas.

MOM: Friends for Christmas? You mean like a Christmas party?

TED: No-o-o, not a party. I want them to come over for Christmas dinner.

MOM: But, Ted, Christmas dinner is family time. You know Granny and Pop always come here for Christmas dinner. And Aunt Christy will be here and her children, of course. Uncle Seth is going to try to make it if he can get a few days off work.

TED: But, Mom, Jonah's family won't have much of a Christmas. They could share with us.

MOM: Why are you so taken with Jonah all of a sudden?

TED: Well, I've been seeing him at school. He doesn't hang out with other guys. He's kind of a loner, I guess.

MOM: Is that the kind of person you want for a friend?

TED: Why not, Mom? He needs a friend. And, Mom, I just found out his dad was laid off. His mom has been too sick to work. He has two little brothers and a sister, and now they are losing their house. They don't have money to make the payments.

Mom: That sounds bad, but Christmas is for family, Ted.

Ted: How would you feel, Mom, if you knew they didn't have enough to eat on Christmas day and we will sit down to a table loaded with good food?

Mom: Well, I don't know.

Ted: Think about it, Mom.

Mom: But our turkey will be just enough for our family. All of them will be here to eat.

Ted: Don't we have money? Can't you just buy another turkey?

Mom: We have money. That's not the point.

Ted: Then what is the point, Mom?

Mom: It's family! Ted! Can't you see that?

Ted: In Sunday school we've been talking about how God gives us so many blessings. Mom, didn't God give us this great family?

Mom: Well, if you put it that way, of course! God gave us everything. I always felt like God brought your dad and me together. It's been such a wonderful relationship—and then you two children came along.

Ted: Then doesn't God want us to share with people who don't have much? Look, Mom, you know what I think? I think God has just given us this opportunity to do something for somebody else. It's like He just dropped it all in my lap and said, "Now what are you going to do with it?"

Mom: Maybe we could buy a turkey and give it to them.

Ted: And not share our time together, our presents and fun?

Mom: Presents? Ted, I'm not going out to buy more presents.

Ted: That's OK, Mom, I'm sure I have more than enough. I'll share mine. *(With head bowed, he starts to walk away.)*

Mom: Wait, Ted. Let me look at this again. You say there are a mom, dad, and four children?

Ted: That's right.

Mom: That will be six extra people. Maybe if I just buy a bigger turkey and maybe add ham to the menu—

Ted: That would be great, Mom! If there is not enough food, I won't ask for seconds of anything.

Mom *(puts her arms around his shoulders):* I don't think it will come to that, Ted.

TED: I probably eat too much anyway.

MOM: Ted, I am going to need you to help me. You figure out what you can about presents. I can give you some things to wrap for them. Maybe we *can* share some of the gifts that you may have been getting. And then we'll have to figure out where all of us can sit to eat our Christmas meal; help me see how we can seat everybody.

TED *(giving MOM a hug):* Thanks, Mom. You won't be sorry.

Scene 2

Scene opens on Christmas Day. Scene includes a decorated tree, a table, chairs, smaller table, etc. MOM and TED are setting the table.

TED: I thought Granny and Pop would be here by now.

MOM: They'll be here.

(Door opens and GRANNY and POP enter.)

GRANNY *(carrying a casserole dish):* Merry Christmas! Here's the potato casserole you wanted me to make. I hope it's good.

POP: Hi, where is everybody?

MOM: They'll be here—just running late.

(Knock on door. TED opens the door and AUNT CHRISTY, BUTCH, JIMMY, and CHRISTINA enter.)

TED: Aunt Christy! *(Gives her a hug.)* Come on in, everybody. Merry Christmas!

DANA *(enters):* Mom, I can't find my . . . I didn't know everybody was already here.

GRANNY: Come here, Sweetie, give your Granny a hug. *(Knock at door.)*

TED *(opens door and JONAH'S family enters):* Hi! I was afraid you decided not to come. I'm so glad you're here now. Look, everybody, I want you to meet my friends. This is Jonah, his mom and dad and his brothers and sister. Jonah, my mom.

JONAH: Hi, Mrs. Tetterton.

MOM *(shaking hands):* Hello, Jonah. I'm glad to meet you.

TED: And my dad.

JONAH: Hi, Mr. Tetterton.

DAD *(shaking hands):* Good to meet you, Jonah.

TED *(pointing):* Dana my sister, Granny, Pop, Aunt Christy, Butch, Jimmy, Christina.

(MOM and DAD and others walk over to shake hands and welcome them. DANA begins talking to JONAH'S SISTER.)

MOM: Listen up, everybody. I know all of you are probably hungry, but we are going to open presents first. We'll just take a short time for that. Then we will eat our Christmas dinner.

DAD: That's a good idea. The first thing we should think about is the gift God gave to everyone when He gave Jesus to be born in Bethlehem. He shared His love and compassion then, and He still shares. Let's think about those things as we share together today. I'd like for us to start with a prayer to thank the Lord. Everybody, please join hands. *(Dad prays.)* God in Heaven, as we come to celebrate the birth of Jesus Your Son, we want to thank You for the greatest gift in all the world. And as we share gifts one with another, help us to see this as a way to share our love for each other. Bless each of us, we pray, in ways that will be beneficial in our lives. In Jesus' name, amen. Now gather around, everybody.

(Gifts are distributed and opened. Laughter and fun are shared. Spend as much time as the director plans.)

MOM: Hey, everyone, it's time to eat. Just find a place to sit, and we'll bring out the food. This is such a happy time. We are so glad to have all of you here. *(Speaking heavenward.)* Thank You, Lord, for this wonderful Christmas.

(She exits. The people begin to sit at various places.)

A Christmas Friend

by LILLIAN ROBBINS

Characters:
    JONATHAN
    FRANK, teen
    MOM
    JOSEPH
    MARY
    INNKEEPER
    FRANK'S FAMILY—Mom, Dad, Sister, Brother, Grandma, Gramps,
        and others (nonspeaking)
    SHEPHERDS, as many as desired
    AARON
    SIMEON
    CHOIR, soloist, or recording

Scene 1: Outside JONATHAN's house

Scene 2: Inside JONATHAN's house

Scene 3: In the church (at the inn)

Scene 4: In the church (at the stable)

Props: Tennis raquet, tree and decorations, bench, chair, Bible, doorbell, blanket, baby, inn door with top that opens separately from bottom, manger with hay, spotlight, seat for MARY

Costumes: long robes or cloaks for Mary and Joseph, Innkeeper's appropriate apparel, Shepherds' robes and crooks

Scene 1

Outside JONATHAN's house, JONATHAN, in a downcast mood, is sitting on a bench. He is talking to himself.

JONATHAN: It is so lonely here. I don't have anybody to talk to. . . . I wonder what Derek is doing now, who he is hanging out with.

FRANK (*enters carrying tennis raquet*): Hi! I just noticed you sitting here, and—are you okay? Something wrong?

JONATHAN: No—I just miss my friends.

FRANK: Where are your friends? Have they gone off somewhere without you?

JONATHAN: They're back in Ohio. My mom and I just moved here.

FRANK: My name is Frank. I go to the school on North Road, but I live just a couple blocks down the street from here.

JONATHAN: I'm Jonathan.

FRANK: I was on my way to the rec center—they have indoor tennis courts. Do you like to play tennis?

JONATHAN: I don't know how, but I guess it could be fun.

FRANK: I don't have to play tennis right now. Maybe we can just talk.

JONATHAN: You're going to stay and talk to me?

FRANK *(sits down):* Sure, why not? Did you have a lot of friends in Ohio?

JONATHAN: Well, you might say so.

FRANK: Tell me about them. Were they boys your age? Were there a lot of neighborhood kids to hang out with?

JONATHAN: The guys were different ages, but my best friend was Derek. He was the best friend in the world. We did things together. We could talk about stuff, and he was always there for me. If I called him to come over, he'd be there in a flash. He could make me laugh—and he knew everything! If I was stumped on homework, he could always help me.

FRANK: Derek sounds like a good friend to have.

JONATHAN: He was the best! Now I'm so lonely, and I can't call him to come over.

FRANK: Well, Christmas is coming soon. You can get excited about that.

JONATHAN: Christmas won't be any fun without Derek! We always got up early on Christmas morning. As soon as we opened our presents, he would come to my house or I'd go over to his place. We'd share our toys, make popcorn, laugh and joke, and just have a good time.

FRANK: Don't you have any friends here, Jonathan?

JONATHAN: Not really. There are guys at school—but they all hang out in groups. I just don't seem to fit in anywhere.

FRANK: How about people in the neighborhood?

JONATHAN: I don't see many. Some guys ride bikes by here, and some skate, but they never stop. *(JONATHAN heaves a sigh.)* I just don't know anyone around here.

FRANK: Do you know Jesus?

JONATHAN: Who?

FRANK: Jesus, you know—you read about Him in the Bible.

JONATHAN: I don't know about that.

FRANK: You don't know about Jesus or you don't know about the Bible?

JONATHAN: I don't really know what you're talking about.

FRANK *(looks up, speaks quietly and earnestly):* Lord, please help me reach Jonathan.

JONATHAN *(looking at Frank):* What did you say?

FRANK: I have a friend I want you to meet. He can be your friend too. He will always be there for you. If you're sad, He finds ways to make you happy. You can call on Him anytime. And, Jonathan, this special friend has an answer for everything.

JONATHAN: He may not want to be my friend. Anyway, nobody can take the place of Derek.

FRANK: This friend will not even want to take the place of Derek. He will just be your special friend. You'll never have to move away and leave Him. He will always be your special friend, even when you grow up and go to college.

JONATHAN *(face brightens):* Who is this friend of yours?

FRANK: His name is Jesus.

JONATHAN: The one you asked me about?

FRANK: That's right, the one I asked you about, and I want you to meet Him right away. I have an idea.

JONATHAN: What kind of idea?

FRANK: I'm going to bring you a Bible and introduce you to Him. And this Sunday night, I'd like you to go with me to a Christmas celebration at church. You will be thrilled when you see the inn at Bethlehem, the stable where the baby lay, the—well, just wait and see. It will be great.

JONATHAN: I don't know that my mom will let me go.

FRANK: She can come too. There will be a lot of adults there. It's for everyone. Gramps and my Grandma always go with us. Actually, they live in another town, but they love this Christmas celebration so much they always come.

JONATHAN: OK. I'll check with my mom.

FRANK: Just remember, Christmas is always a happy time when you put Jesus right smack in the middle of it. This may be the very best Christmas you ever had.

JONATHAN: What about presents? Do we have to bring presents?

FRANK: No, you just need to be there. Don't worry. You'll see. *(Frank prepares to leave.)* I'll be back and bring you a Bible. Maybe I can meet your mom then. *(Walks away.)*

JONATHAN *(goes toward FRANK)*: Frank, wait up. What should I wear to this Christmas celebration you're talking about?

FRANK: Just regular clothes. What you're wearing now is fine. *(Walking away.)* See you, Jonathan.

JONATHAN: Yeah, see you.

Scene 2

In JONATHAN'S family room, MOM is decorating the tree. Most of the decorations are already on: outlandish, colorful beads, garlands, etc. Wrapped Christmas boxes are stacked around the tree.

JONATHAN *(enters)*: Hey, Mom, did you see that guy who was just talking to me?

MOM *(continues decorating)*: No, I didn't see anyone. I've been busy decorating this tree. Still got a lot more to do. You know we always get our tree up earlier than this, but with the moving and everything, it's really late this year.

JONATHAN: I think the guy is pretty cool. His name is Frank. He goes to that school out on North Road.

MOM: Really?

JONATHAN: Yeah, he was on his way to play tennis, but he stopped to talk to me. I was surprised. Most people seem too busy to notice me, much less stop to talk.

MOM: That's nice.

JONATHAN: He's kinda big. But he doesn't act all arrogant and stuff—just a regular guy.

(Mom doesn't respond.)

JONATHAN *(emphatically)*: Mom, are you listening to me?

MOM *(looking at him)*: Oh, sure, do you want something?

JONATHAN: Just to have you talk to me. I don't have anybody to talk to since we moved. Frank is the first person who has even told me his name.

MOM: Frank? Who is Frank?

JONATHAN: I was just telling you—the guy who stopped by out there to talk to me.

Mom: What did he want?

Jonathan: He didn't want anything. He was just being friendly.

Mom *(starts back to the tree):* That's good.

Jonathan *(taking her hand):* Mom, wait a minute!

Mom: Jonathan, you know I have so much to do. I've got to finish this tree, wrap two or three more boxes, fix our supper—

Jonathan: But, Mom, I need you to listen to me. I have more to tell you —about what Frank said. Come sit down for just one minute, please.

Mom *(moving to sofa):* Oh, all right; just one minute then!

Jonathan: See, Mom, I was telling Frank about Derek, how much I miss him . . .

Mom: I know, Jonathan, I miss my old friends too. But it'll get better after a while.

Jonathan: Anyway, Frank . . . *(doorbell rings).* I'll get it. *(Opens door, Frank enters.)* Hi, Frank. You came back just as you said you would.

FRANK: I live just two blocks down the street. It didn't take long.

JONATHAN: Come on in. This is my mom. We were just talking about you.

FRANK *(extending hand):* Good to meet you, Mrs.—-Ah?

MOM: Mrs. Averis. Likewise, good to meet you.

FRANK: My, what a big Christmas tree! And so colorful!

MOM: I know. People always say I have the strangest looking Christmas tree. But I like it this way. I don't care for lights, but I like color.

JONATHAN: Our tree always looks different from everybody else's.

FRANK: And so many presents! You must have a very big family or a lot of friends.

MOM *(laughing):* Actually, it's neither. I just like it to seem like a lot of presents. I wrap empty boxes and just stack them all around. I'm pretty good at pretending.

FRANK: You seem to be enjoying it.

MOM: Well . . .

JONATHAN: Mom's busy all the time, though. She almost never sits down.

FRANK: I told Jonathan I would bring him a Bible. I wanted to get it to him right away so he could read some before Sunday night.

MOM: I have a Bible around here somewhere.

FRANK: I thought Jonathan might like to have one of his own. Actually, this is the Bible I used to read and study, but I want Jonathan to have it. *(Hands it over to Jonathan)*

JONATHAN *(taking the Bible):* But, Frank, if this is your book, I don't want to take it away from you.

FRANK: Jonathan, this is not just a *book*. It's more special than any book you will ever read. And I can get another one for me.

MOM: I don't know that Jonathan will care to read it.

FRANK: You might be surprised. As I was telling Jonathan, Sunday night is the time for our special Christmas celebration at church. I was hoping you and Jonathan could go with our family.

JONATHAN: Frank, I haven't had a chance to talk to Mom about that yet.

MOM *(getting up):* I've got to get back to work. You two can talk on as much as you like.

JONATHAN: That's the way it is—always. She never has time to talk.

FRANK: Let's just sit here a minute. My time is your time, and I want to show you here in the Bible where you can read about the first Christmas.

(MOM is busy with the tree but occasionally stops to listen.)

JONATHAN: It's such a big book.

FRANK: True, but it's in sections so it's easy to read just the part you want to read at anytime. *(Opens Bible)* Now here is the book of Luke. See? I've written down the part I'd like you to read before Sunday. When you read this part, you'll see how an angel appeared to a woman named Mary. The angel said Mary was going to have a baby boy, and His name would be Jesus. *(Turns to Luke 2)* When you read on into this chapter, you'll read about the first Christmas.

JONATHAN: That looks like a lot to read.

FRANK: Not really. Just remember that God loves all of us, and that includes you, Jonathan. He loves us so much He sent His Son to earth to save us.

JONATHAN: I'm not sure I'll understand all this.

FRANK: If you'll just read this in the Bible, when you see the Christmas pageant, it will seem more real. And, Jonathan, if there is anything you don't understand, you and I can talk about it. *(Stands up to go)* I'd better get going now. See you, Jonathan. So long, Mrs. Averis.

MOM: Bye, Frank. See you.

(FRANK leaves. MOM comes over to JONATHAN, who already has started to read.)

MOM: What about this Christmas celebration you two were talking about?

JONATHAN: It's at their church. Frank said we can go with his family.

MOM: How much does it cost?

JONATHAN: I don't think it's something you pay for. Frank didn't say anything about money. When I asked him if we need to take presents, he said, "Just be there." Frank says it's great and I want to go.

MOM: Well, I guess if I get all my work caught up, unpack all those other boxes, find something decent to wear—

JONATHAN: Mom, just go! That's all you have to do!

Scene 3

FRANK'S family, JONATHAN, and MRS. AVERIS come and sit in front of the auditorium. Seats will be reserved. On stage are bales of hay and front of an inn with split door so top half can open separately from bottom.

JOSEPH (*enters helping* MARY *along*): You can sit right here, Mary. I'll put this blanket over the hay. It will be more comfortable than riding the donkey over those long, bumpy paths. (*Spreads blanket for* MARY *to sit on.*) I won't be long, Mary. I just have to get a place for us to sleep tonight.

(*JOSEPH goes to door and knocks, no answer; knocks again with no answer; knocks again harder, and the top door opens.*)

INNKEEPER: What do you want?

JOSEPH: My wife and I need a place to sleep.

INNKEEPER: The inn is full. (*Starts to close door.*)

JOSEPH: No, wait! There is my wife over there. (*Pointing*) As you can see, she is expecting a child, maybe even tonight. We must have a place.

INNKEEPER: You came to Bethlehem for the taxing as Caesar Augustus demanded?

JOSEPH: Yes, we are of the lineage of David.

INNKEEPER: Where did you come from?

JOSEPH: Nazareth of Galilee. It has been a very long journey for Mary.

INNKEEPER: I would think so. But why didn't you come earlier in the day before all the rooms were filled?

JOSEPH: We couldn't travel very fast. We had to make several stops along the way for Mary. If your wife ever had children, you know how it is.

INNKEEPER: Yes, of course. I wish there was something I could do, but I can't very well ask someone to give up his room for you.

JOSEPH: But there must be a place. I know there is a way. The Lord would not just leave us out in the cold. I just don't know right now what to do.

MARY (*calling out, her discomfort obvious*): Joseph!

JOSEPH: Yes, Mary, I'll be there. (*To the* INNKEEPER) You see how it is. Where can I find a place for Mary to stay tonight?

INNKEEPER: I know of only one place. You could go down to the stable. There is plenty of fresh hay there. You could make a bed for her in the stable. I know that's not much to offer, but at least she would have shelter and a place to lie down.

JOSEPH: Yes, you are right.

INNKEEPER: Just lead your donkey right down that way. (*Points*) There is plenty of room for your donkey too and you can feed him some of the hay.

JOSEPH: Thank you. We'll go right along. *(JOSEPH returns to MARY and together they leave.)*

INNKEEPER: I wonder if Caesar Augustus will ever know how much of a burden he has put on our people by requiring them to go back to their hometowns. If he had just arranged for the listing to be done in the towns where the people live, this poor young woman wouldn't be in this situation now in a strange city here in Bethlehem.

Scene 4

Spotlight on the manger scene. MARY sits beside manger where the baby lies. JOSEPH stands nearby.

JOSEPH: Mary, are you all right?

MARY: Yes, Joseph. Thank you for your concern. But now I want to hold Him, my precious little boy.

(JOSEPH lifts the baby out of the manger and places Him in MARY's lap.)

JOSEPH: This is a very special little boy, Mary. We knew because the angel told us you would give birth to God's Son, but we could never be certain just how it would come to pass, especially having to travel here from Nazareth.

MARY: But we always knew God would take care of us, Joseph. I think our Son has such a beautiful name, the name the angel said to give Him, Jesus. It sounds like music when I say it—Jesus.

JOSEPH: I remember when the angel said to me, "Call his name Jesus"—Savior—"for he shall save his people from their sins" (Matthew 1:21).

MARY: It's the fulfillment of Isaiah's prophecy: "'They shall call his name Immanuel,' which being interpreted is, God with us" (Matthew 1:23).

JOSEPH: *(touches the face of the baby)* Mary, can you imagine, God with us! What a wonderful miracle God has given to us and to all people from this day forward.

MARY: We must thank the Lord God for providing this place for Jesus to be born. I am really content and happy. We were never alone, you know. God was always with us.

(JOSEPH puts the baby back in the manger. Spotlight dims.)

SOLOIST: "O Holy Night"

(As a bright light shines in the distance, voices are heard.)

SIMEON: Look, Aaron, look at that light!
AARON: What is it? What does it mean? What should we do?
SIMEON: I don't know. It's frightening!
ANGEL: Don't be afraid. I've come to bring you good news which will be to all people. For unto you is born this day a Savior which is Christ the Lord. You will find the baby in Bethlehem where he lies in a manger, wrapped in swaddling clothes.
SIMEON: Did you hear? A Savior is born in Bethlehem!

CHOIR: "Angels We Have Heard on High"

AARON: We must go and see this baby. We'll just walk across the hills and look all through the city until we find Him.
SIMEON: In a manger, the angel said.
AARON: Yes, lying in a manger.

SOLOIST: "What Child Is This?"

(Lights come on in the manger scene again.)

SINGERS: "While Shepherds Watched Their Flocks"

(SHEPHERDS come in through the audience to the stage. They kneel at the manger. JOSEPH gives the baby to MARY again. As she holds Him, she sings "Away in a Manger.")
MARY: "Away in a Manger"

(Finale: All characters come on stage. JONATHAN speaks to FRANK.)

JONATHAN: You're right, Frank, this is the greatest Christmas I ever had. Now I know what Christmas is all about. What do you think, Mom?
MOM: I think it's wonderful! Thanks Frank, for helping us experience the true meaning of Christmas.

ALL: "Joy to the World!"

Busy, Busy Christmas

by KAREN LEET

Summary: This is a performance poem that may be read or recited as a group or with individual assigned parts. Costumes and motions may be added as desired.

Hurry here, hurry there,
Hurry, hurry everywhere.
Christmas is coming, coming fast.
Put up the tree!
Hang the lights!
Bake more cookies!
Buy some presents!
Wrap them nicely!
Sing some carols!
Watch Christmas movies!
So much to do!

Hurry here, hurry there,
Hurry, hurry everywhere.
Rush and fuss. So much to do!
Hurry here, hurry there,
Hurry, hurry everywhere.
Wait a moment. Be still and see
all that Christmas is meant to be.
Stop the hurry! Stop the rush!
Shh, wait a moment. Shh, hush.
Listen for the sound of angels singing—
feel the joy baby Jesus is bringing.

The Night the King Slept in a Stable

by ELAINE INGALLS HOGG

Summary: An earthly king learns of a heavenly King and is asked to make a response to Him.

Characters:
EMPEROR AUGUSTUS
FIRST SERVANT
SECOND SERVANT—a younger boy
SERVANTS—nonspeaking parts

Setting: a room in the emperor's palace—the furniture is patched and shabby in appearance and the wallpaper is hanging off the wall

Props: throne, table, shabby robe for the emperor, one velvet trimmed robe with fur and gold braid, mirror, feather duster, treasure chest, colored gem or two, coins and paper money stored in the treasure chest, scroll for the decree, stemmed glasses, candles, fine dinnerware

Running Time: 12-15 minutes

Scene One

EMPEROR AUGUSTUS wanders around the room, touching the patched furniture and pointing out the run-down state of his palace.

EMPEROR AUGUSTUS: Look at this! No man in my position should have to live like this! It's no better than a pigpen! Since when does an emperor, the most important person in the land, live in a dump and wear shabby clothes? Look at me! There's not a speck of gold trim anywhere. An important person like me should have gold on his clothes.

FIRST SERVANT: [*rubbing his hands together in a nervous motion*] Sir, I agree! You do need to remodel this place, and you definitely need to buy more clothes!

EMPEROR AUGUSTUS: [*to his servant*] Find my treasure chest and bring it

Skits and Plays for Children

to me right away. I'm going to order new clothes—fine velvet robes trimmed with furs and gold—more gold than any other leader in the world.

[FIRST SERVANT *hurries out of the room and returns with the treasure chest.* EMPEROR AUGUSTUS *takes the chest and empties the contents on the table. Slowly he counts his money—piling it into neat stacks on the table. When he is finished counting, he shakes his head.*]

FIRST SERVANT: Is there a problem?

EMPEROR AUGUSTUS: Is there a problem? Of course, there's a problem! There isn't enough money here to buy Dick Whittington's cat a new pair of boots, let alone renovate this place or build a bigger palace. There isn't even enough money to buy one new suit, let alone one trimmed in gold. An important emperor like me needs at least 20 new suits trimmed with gold. [*He thrusts the coins and money back in the chest, slams the lid, and stands to his feet.*] I need more money! [*He paces around the room, rubs his brow as if thinking.*] I know what I'll do. Bring me my pen and a scroll! I'll tell everyone in my kingdom to go to the town where he was born and write his name in the scroll there.

FIRST SERVANT: But sir, some of the people will have to travel for days to add their names to a scroll.

EMPEROR AUGUSTUS: [*laughs out loud*] Don't you think I know that? But I'm the boss, and I'm telling them to come to the town of their births and add their names to my scroll. That is that!

[EMPEROR AUGUSTUS *stomps towards the door as if to go out of the room. When he reaches the door, he stops and orders* FIRST SERVANT *to fetch all the other servants in the palace.* FIRST SERVANT *scurries out, bowing and hustling.* EMPEROR AUGUSTUS *circles the room and settles himself on his throne. When* FIRST SERVANT *returns, he has several other servants with him.*]

EMPEROR AUGUSTUS: Listen to my instructions! I have an important message I want to send out to my subjects. Tomorrow morning you will go to all towns and villages in the land and take this message. Put up signs saying, "Emperor Augustus has declared that every family must go to the town where they were born and put their names in the big book there." They think I want to count them but what I really want to do is get their addresses, and then I can send them a big tax bill. *[Rubs his hands in glee.]* When I get all that money, I'll be the richest man on earth. Soon I'll have the nicest clothes and the biggest palace in all the land.

Scene Two

EMPEROR AUGUSTUS is eating his dinner and SECOND SERVANT comes up to him.

SECOND SERVANT: Excuse me, sir. I have news for you.

EMPEROR AUGUSTUS: Who has been teaching you your manners? *[Roars at the little one. SECOND SERVANT trembles but stays near the table.]*

SECOND SERVANT: But this is very important, sir!

EMPEROR AUGUSTUS: I'm eating my dinner. If it isn't serious, I'll see you get a flogging.

SECOND SERVANT: It is serious, sir! Very serious! I have heard some news and I'm sure you want to hear it too.

EMPEROR AUGUSTUS: News, you say? Do tell!

[EMPEROR AUGUSTUS slams his fork on table, wipes face with napkin, and stands directly in front of SECOND SERVANT but SECOND SERVANT doesn't back away.]

SECOND SERVANT: You always say you are the most important person in the whole land, but I heard someone say that you aren't as important as you think you are.

[EMPEROR AUGUSTUS's face turns red, and he wipes his face with his napkin. He stands up as tall as he can stand.]

EMPEROR AUGUSTUS: *[in a loud voice]* Who in his right mind would ever say I'm not the most important person in these parts, if not the whole world?

SECOND SERVANT: Shepherds, sir. Some shepherds were getting water for their sheep this morning, and they said that you aren't as important as you think you are!

Skits and Plays for Children

EMPEROR AUGUSTUS: [laughs uproariously] Shepherds! Servant boy, who do you think you are talking to?

SECOND SERVANT: Sir, the shepherds said they were tending their sheep in a field near the town of Bethlehem. All at once the sky lit up with a strange light. They were so scared that they hid behind some bushes near the stream. Then they heard a noise in the sky. When they dared to look up at the sky, they saw a choir of angels. The angels were saying, "Glory to God in the highest, and on earth peace to men on whom his favor rests."

EMPEROR AUGUSTUS: Hmm! Shepherds! Angels! That must have been one outstanding party or else they were dreaming. Everyone knows that all the shepherds in the world aren't as important as an emperor. Go away and don't bother me. I'm busy. [Waves his hand in a signal of dismissal.]

SECOND SERVANT: [backs away as if to leave and then decides against it] But sir, the angel said the only Son of the one true God was born last night in Bethlehem.

EMPEROR AUGUSTUS: Where? There are no palaces in Bethlehem. It's the smallest town in Judah!

SECOND SERVANT: The baby wasn't born in a palace. He wasn't born in a hotel either. The innkeeper said they were all booked up.

EMPEROR AUGUSTUS: Huh! Where was He born? A barn?

SECOND SERVANT: Why sir, how did you ever guess? All the hotels were full. There was some sort of convention in town. The town was full of people who came to town to add their names to a scroll.

EMPEROR AUGUSTUS: [raises eyebrows and shows a little more interest in what the servant is telling him] How did the shepherds know where to find this baby?

SECOND SERVANT: The angel gave them a sign so they would know which baby was God's Son.

EMPEROR AUGUSTUS: [laughs] Ha! A sign! Did someone paint a sign and put it in front of the barn saying "God's Son Was Born Here"? Is this some kind of joke?

SECOND SERVANT: No sir, no sir, no joke. The angel said, "This will be a sign to you: You will find a baby wrapped in cloths and lying in a manger."

EMPEROR AUGUSTUS: [wanders around the room and then climbs onto his throne] God would never allow His Son to be born in a barn. No one would put strips of cloth on a king! They would only wrap the Son of God in linen or silk. This is a foolish story. Why, God would only invite kings and queens and emperors to the birth of His Son. People like me.

SECOND SERVANT: *[crossing the room and standing in front of the throne]* That's not what the shepherds said.

EMPEROR AUGUSTUS: Shepherds! Phooey on shepherds!

SECOND SERVANT: But sir! The shepherds have proof! They found the baby. He was wrapped in strips of cloth and lying in a manger, just like the angels had said.

EMPEROR AUGUSTUS: What nonsense!

SECOND SERVANT: *[in a hesitant manner]* Sir, the shepherds said something else too.

EMPEROR AUGUSTUS: *[lets us know he is agitated by the tone of his voice]* What? What did they say?

SECOND SERVANT: Your Honor, the ancient Scriptures say He is the Son of God. Besides, not even King Herod had angels singing when he was born.

EMPEROR AUGUSTUS: The very idea! The Son of God . . . born in a barn . . . in Bethlehem? Impossible!

[Then EMPEROR AUGUSTUS drops his head in his hands as if to think about what he has heard. Finally he looks up and he speaks to his servant] What do the Holy Scriptures say?

SECOND SERVANT: A long time ago the prophet Micah wrote that even though Bethlehem was the smallest clan it was going to be the birthplace of someone who will be ruler over Israel. *[After a slight pause]* Sir I believe the shepherds and the Holy Scriptures. Last night there was no room at the inn so the King of kings slept in a stable. Sir, are you more generous than the innkeeper? Will you make room for the King of kings?

[Blackout.]

I Have a Christmas Message

by DIXIE PHILLIPS

Costumes: costumes for angel, shepherd, and wise man

Three children enter.

ANGEL:

I have a Christmas message of joy.
Such good news! It's a baby boy!

SHEPHERD:

I have a Christmas message too.
He was born for me and you.
[points to congregation]

WISE MAN:

I have a Christmas message to share.
God's gift is the grandest gift anywhere!

Poems
and Readings
for Teens
and Adults

The Bells of Christmas
by Douglas Raymond Rose

Hear the bells of Christmas
Ringing loud and clear—
Ringing in the love of God
For all the poor and dear.
Hear the bells of Christmas
Ringing out across the snow—
Ringing in true peace on earth
Ringing out resentments old.
Hear the bells of Christmas
Ringing in hope that's true—
Ring O bells of Christmas
Ring out the old; ring in the new.

Christmas
by Alyce Pickett

Sing a carol, trim the tree;
Wrap a gift, or two, or three.
Hang a wreath outside the door;
Bake the cookies—bake some more.
Share with friends and with the poor
Your goodies and good will. Be sure
And remember on this date
The reason why we celebrate.

The Light of Christmas
by Dolores Steger

The light of Christmas shines in me,
And Jesus is its flame,
With love and hope and faithfulness,
I bow before His name.

Unto Us
by Dolores Steger

Unto us a child is born,
A Savior and a Son
Whose name shall be Emmanuel,
God with us, every one.
Counselor and prince of peace,
By us He shall be called,
And on the throne of Father God,
He will there be installed.
And worlds will recognize Him by
The light to hearts He brings,
And bow before Him, crowned
    with love,
As Lord, the King of kings.

King of Kings
by Dolores Steger

A manger cold, a manger bare,
A baby, tender, lying there.
A shepherd bows before the boy,
A Wise Man gives a gift with joy,
An angel smiles and flutters
    wings,
And all adore the King of kings.

The Blessing of Love
by Dolores Steger

The shepherds on hillsides
Are tending their sheep,
While in Bethlehem,
There's a baby asleep.

The angels are waiting,
The good news to tell,
While the child calmly rests,
In slumber's sweet spell.

The Magi now follow
A star in the skies,
While in a soft manger,
A dear baby lies.

All people, it's Christmas,
God's gift from above,
While in swaddling clothes,
Reigns the blessing of love.

God's Gift
by Alyce Pickett

The shepherds saw bright angels . . .
Listened to them sing
Songs of praise to God above
For a new born king.

Then the shepherds left their sheep
Because angels had said,
"You'll find the Christ-child baby
In Bethlehem's manger bed."

They hurried then to find the babe . . .
The Messiah God had given,
They found and praised the holy child,
A special gift from Heaven.

What a glorious, wondrous time,
This night of Jesus' birth!
All the love Heaven possessed
Came with God's Son to earth!

Embrace Me with Christmas

by Elaine Hardt

Embrace me with Christmas,
enfold me in love,
as snowflakes drift softly
from gray skies above.

Surround me with cheer;
let the music begin,
a heavenly chorus
resounding again.

Festive lights shine,
scented candles aglow.
A hush fills my heart
as I seek to know:

Is it still possible
to truly believe?
Is it too late
for me to receive?

And then, truth dawns
with His magnificent grace,
a marvel of blessing
in our Savior's face.

Such glory descends,
human eye cannot see.
His holy presence
whispers peace within me.

Skits, Plays, and Dramas for Teens and Adults

Unstoppable Spirit

by JOHN COSPER

Summary: Construction workers find the true meaning of Christmas in spite of having to work on Christmas Eve.

Characters:

> BURT—construction worker, middle-age man, very cheerful and filled with the joy of the Lord
>
> ROD—construction worker, middle-age man, cynical and bitter about having to work on the holidays

Setting: road with roadblocks, road cones, and construction signs

Props: orange cones, STOP/SLOW sign, bicycle horn to honk backstage to mimic a car horn, construction signs, road blocks

Costumes: winter construction worker gear and hardhats

BURT stands on stage, bundled up for cold weather with a hard hat. He stands by an orange cone with a pole coming out of it. Atop the pole is a STOP/SLOW sign with the STOP sign facing the audience.

BURT: OK, folks. *[turns the sign to slow]* Happy driving! Keep it slow, keep it safe. Merry Christmas! *[waves]* Hi there, little fella. Merry Christmas! *[waves]* Hi, folks. Keep it slow. Hi—Oh, that's not a nice gesture, but God still loves you.

[ROD walks over, shivering in his big coat.]

ROD: Man, can you believe this? Calling us out to work on Christmas Eve?

BURT: It's all part of the job, Rod.

ROD: Yeah, but making us work on Christmas Eve? It's not our fault the boys were digging in the wrong spot all week! Why do we all have to suffer for their mistake? Merry Christmas, ha! I have two bicycles and a computer to assemble, Burt. I'm gonna be up til 5 AM.

BURT: I hear you. I have a dollhouse and some kind of space warrior to build. Merry Christmas!

ROD: Man, how do you do it?

BURT: Well, tonight, I figure I'll drink a lot of caffeine.

ROD: No, Burt. I mean you and your Merry Christmas spirit. Twenty guys are out here with us, freezing our tails off, and you're smiling like a kid who just saw Santa!

BURT: I have so much to be thankful for. I have a job with a good paycheck. And I'm earning overtime working the holiday. *[waves to another car]* Merry Christmas!

ROD: You don't strike me as the money-motivated type.

BURT: No, but I also have a loving family waiting for me at home and we have the love of Jesus.

ROD: Say that again.

BURT: Which part?

ROD: The Jesus part.

BURT: We have the love of Jesus to celebrate at Christmas. You do know Jesus is the reason for Christmas, right?

ROD: Sure I do. It's just that's the first time I ever heard anyone but a preacher say it.

BURT: You don't have to be a preacher to say that. Doesn't matter what your job is, you can do it for the Lord. And when you consider all He has done for us, well . . . it's hard not to praise Him all the time.

ROD: You're a strange one, Burt. I've known a lot of fellas call themselves Christian over the years, and I've never seen one act like you do. Most of them would just complain as much as the rest of us.

BURT: The Lord has blessed me, and no matter what—

[BURT turns the sign to stop. Horn blares and he waves.]

BURT: I can't help but praise God. I'm only sorry that more Christians don't do the same so you could believe it.

ROD: Don't be sorry, Burt. Seeing one true believer like you makes me more than a little curious.

[Blackout.]

The Season for the Reason

by CAROL S. REDD

Summary: Searching for the Christmas spirit.
Characters:
- TAMMY—exhausted Christmas shopper
- STACY—exhausted Christmas shopper
- FAYE—exhausted Christmas shopper
- A. J.—volunteer helping to set up the community nativity scene
- VALERIE—young, homeless girl

Setting: outside on a park bench

Props: park bench, filled shopping bags for three Christmas shoppers, manger scene

Costumes: winter clothes for shoppers and volunteer worker, tattered dress and sweater for homeless girl

As drama begins, VALERIE, dressed as a homeless person, walks slowly on stage and sits on park bench as if cold and sad. She shivers and tries to pull tattered sweater around her. As TAMMY and STACY approach the bench they suddenly stop and look disapprovingly at VALERIE. VALERIE looks intimidated and quickly exits.

TAMMY: *[gesturing towards VALERIE]* I'm sick of seeing these homeless people hanging around the mall. Why don't they just go get a job? And if I have to go in one more store and listen to one more fish on a wall singing "Jingle Bells" I think I'm just going to scream!

STACY: Whoa . . . sounds like somebody has already lost their Christmas spirit!

TAMMY: Christmas spirit? I haven't had that for so many years, I'm not even sure I'd recognize it!

STACY: Oh, I know what you mean . . . the holidays aren't really the same for me anymore either. It used to be a lot of fun . . . but that was a long time ago. Now it's pretty much just stress, bills, and a lot of unnecessary work. *[pause]* Well, anyway, I'm glad we set up a meeting time to take a break. We have to wait on Faye anyway . . . she's running a little late . . . probably trapped in one of the checkout lines. I can't believe how crowded the stores are!

A.J.: *[enters carrying manger]* Pardon me ladies . . . we're putting up the community nativity over there *[gestures to off-stage area]* and I was just going to set this manger here by the bench while we set up the stable. I don't want it to get broken. One of the men in my church made it. I can't tell you how much time he invested in this—kind of a labor of love you might say. I'd feel terrible if anything happened to it. Will it be in your way if I put it over here?

Tammy: No, that's fine . . .

Stacy: We're only going to be a few minutes anyway. No problem.

Tammy: *[kind of mumbling]* Not that I wouldn't like to just sit here until spring . . .

Stacy: What's the matter Tammy? I thought it would be fun for us all to do our Christmas shopping together . . . but you seem so depressed.

Tammy: It's just that there's too much to do! My husband volunteered me to fix Christmas dinner for the whole family this year! Can you believe that?

Stacy: Well can't you just make it simple? How about a buffet . . . or have it catered?

Tammy: Oh, no! We must have a homemade turkey dinner for Christmas day—it's *tradition*! I've never fixed a turkey in my whole life . . . not even a little one! And every time I asked someone for the best way to do it, I get a different answer . . . under a foil tent, wrapped in cheesecloth, in a cooking bag, in a brown paper bag, upside down, standing on end, inside out and . . .

Stacy: Inside out?

Tammy: OK, maybe that was a slight exaggeration. But, believe it or not, I'm already on a first name basis with the people who answer phones for the "turkey hotline!" Christmas is bad enough as it is, but just the thought of this dinner is making me physically ill . . .

Stacy: Oh, here comes Faye . . . *[speaking in direction of Faye]* . . . Where have you been? We thought you had gotten lost.

Faye: *[carrying two shopping bags]* Not lost . . . just going crazy trying to find the "perfect" gift for everyone on my list . . . and guess what . . . it didn't happen!

Tammy: Well, it looks like you did all right to me.

Faye: Oh, this stuff? These are just some things I picked up for myself. I couldn't find anything for anyone else. Everything I liked, I couldn't

Skits, Plays, and Dramas for Teens and Adults

afford and everything I could afford, I didn't like. I think Christmas is completely overrated. I don't want to sound like Scrooge, but I would be much happier if we never celebrated Christmas again. *[noticing the manger]* What's that?

TAMMY: It's a manger for the community nativity. One of the guys put the manger over here so nothing would happen to it while they set up the stable and all. *[looking in distance in direction of where man walked]* Wait a minute. It looks like the nativity is finished, doesn't it?

STACY: It sure does . . . and those guys have all left. I guess they set everything up and totally forgot the manger was over here . . . that's pretty weird.

FAYE: It sure is. How could you possibly go to all that trouble and leave out one of the most important parts?

TAMMY: Actually, it's probably the most important part. Without Jesus there wouldn't even be a Christmas.

STACY: I think those guys completely missed the point! *[gesturing to the manger]* What were they thinking?

FAYE: That's just it . . . they obviously *weren't* thinking. Probably in too much of a hurry to put up the rest of the Christmas decorations.

TAMMY: Well, speaking of Christmas . . . let's get going. I still have *a million* things to do.

STACY: Yeah . . . me too. I can't wait until the holidays are over.

FAYE: Me neither. Bring on January!

[After all have exited, VALERIE returns to the bench and sits on the side opposite the manger and slowly moves toward it. Then she touches the baby and appears to wipe away her tears. She removes her sweater and places it over the baby, and slowly exits. Blackout.]

Charlie's Christmas Wish

by JOHN COSPER

Summary: A homeless man observes people at Christmas and how so few get the true spirit of Christmas.

Characters:

    CHARLIE—a homeless man

    TOM & LYNN—parents shopping for their children

    CHRIS, BRANDI & MELINDA—teenagers

    PAUL—another homeless man

Setting: Modern day, a busy street

Props: shopping bags, receipts

Costumes: old, worn out clothes for CHARLIE and PAUL; modern dress for the rest

TOM and LYNN enter carrying large shopping bags each. LYNN is looking at a handful of receipts. CHARLIE, who wears old looking clothes looks quite haggard, enters unnoticed.

TOM: *[looks over LYNN's shoulder]* Let's see. Are we evened up yet?

LYNN: It looks like we're OK on Jan and Casey, but we're $20 short on Brian.

TOM: Ooh! I know just the thing! He's been crazy about the Dallas Cowboys ever since we went to that game with the McDaniel's in September. I saw a Cowboys football at—

[TOM and LYNN almost run into CHARLIE at center stage. They both look up just in time and are startled. They excuse themselves and continue on around him towards the stage left exit. TOM glances at CHARLIE. CHARLIE watches them.]

TOM: *[as if nothing had happened]* I saw a Cowboys football in the toy store. We can stop by there on our way home.

LYNN: Perfect.

[TOM and LYNN exit.]

CHARLIE: You know, it never changes. Parents running around at the last minute to even up their kids' wish lists.

[CHARLIE sits down.]

CHARLIE: I can still remember sitting up all night with my brother dreaming of that special Christmas toy: bikes, trains, dolls—*[as if the last comment was a joke]* no, wait, forget I said dolls. I'll tell you what, I never grow tired of watching the beaming faces of little kids on their way to see Santa Claus. I always look forward to Christmas. Of course, I don't enjoy the cold that comes with it, but even on the coldest nights, when the only bed I have is a snowy sidewalk, I can lose myself in the lights and decorations. There's something extra special about Christmas. Everyone becomes filled with love and goodwill for his fellow man. More people volunteer to work the local soup kitchen or donate food and clothes to the shelters.

[CHRIS, BRANDI, and MELINDA enter; girls are giggling.]

CHRIS: So anyway, the bum walks up to Santa Claus and goes, "Hey, man, I don't think you should let that one reindeer drive." Santa said, "Why not?"

[BRANDI and MELINDA see CHARLIE, look at each other.]

CHRIS: Because his nose is redder than mine! *[laughs]*
BRANDI: Umm, Chris? *[points to CHARLIE]*
CHRIS: *[sees CHARLIE, then says]* Oh . . . hi, there. *[pulls out a dollar and says in a condescending tone]* Here you go, man. Merry Christmas!

[BRANDI and MELINDA exit laughing. CHRIS follows.]

CHARLIE: Everybody's full of goodwill. Everybody thinks they can solve *all* your problems with a few bucks but they're missing it. I guess that's why Jesus talked about looking at the world through the eyes of a child. I already have the answer to all my problems. It is more powerful than money and more real than goodwill. I have Jesus. And Jesus is more than just a once-a-year thing. He's my Savior the whole year round—not just in December.

[CHARLIE *stands up.* PAUL *enters, shivering like he's cold, and sits off to the side.*]

CHARLIE: When others walk by, all they see is a dirty bum. God sees my heart. I'm thankful He does because what He sees inside of me is beautiful. I'll bet when you first saw me, you thought you were going to hear me talk about how miserable I am. That's not what I'm about. I'm just an ordinary man in an extraordinary situation. But no matter where I go, or who I become, I know Jesus loves me. He can use me just as well as he can use you to reach out and tell someone that He loves them.

[CHARLIE *hands* PAUL *the money* CHRIS *gave him, then exits. Blackout.*]

The Forgotten Child

by LORI STANLEY ROELEVELD

Summary: ZACK is a teenage boy living in a state-run group home. He is forgotten by his family on Christmas Eve and must spend it with MATTHEW, a Christian staff worker. They make several stops on the way home, through which MATTHEW shows ZACK the relevance of the Christmas story.

Characters:

    MATTHEW—Christian staff worker in a group home for troubled teens, late 20s

    ZACK—angry resident of the home with no place to go for Christmas, teenager

    NARRATOR—to read Scripture

    GABRIEL, MARY, JOSEPH, INNKEEPER, SHEPHERDS, AND ANGELS—non-speaking parts for any ages

Setting: driving place to place in a small town: half the stage is a car, half the stage will change from group home to a still scene of the Christmas story

Props: driver and passenger seats of a car, desk, telephone, two chairs, backpack or duffle bag, church pew

Costumes: modern clothes for MATT and ZACK, Bible-times costumes for nativity scene members

---

MATTHEW is seated at the desk on the phone. ZACK is slumped in the chair fiddling with a backpack or duffel bag.

MATTHEW: *[hanging up the phone]* Zack, I've tried every place I can think of but no one's seen your uncle today.

ZACK: *[angrily]* No kidding. I told you he'd forget. Probably got drunk on the way here.

MATTHEW: I'm sorry, kid. This is no way for you to celebrate Christmas Eve. Look, you're welcome to hang out with me tonight and tomorrow. My shift is done and, now that everyone else is gone, we can take off. I've already cleared it with your social worker; *[joyfully]* so you're set

---

to ring in Christmas with me.

ZACK: No way! I'm not interested in celebrating any part of this stupid holiday. Maybe Christmas makes you all warm and fuzzy but it's just another day for me. I never did believe in Santa and no one's asking for my Christmas list! I got no home and my family—well, my drunk uncle was the best hope I had of even getting dinner. Thanks but I'm sure you've got a little family to go to yourself or some big party or whatever.

MATTHEW: I do have a few stops to make tonight but you can come along with me. You've actually got no choice. I ain't much but I'm all you've got tonight so you may as well make the best of it.

[ZACK shrugs his shoulders and picks up his duffel bag. MATTHEW puts on his coat, turns off the lights. They leave the office and head out to the car. The other half of the stage is set as a tableau of Gabriel's appearance to MARY and JOSEPH's dreams.]

MATTHEW: Now, who told you Christmas was about families and home? Did no one ever tell you how Christmas started or did you just forget?

ZACK: Oh, don't start! If you're gonna pull out a Bible and tell me about baby Jesus, no thanks! That story has about as much to do with this day and age as black and white TV. I'll hang with you but I'm not into Jesus and He sure ain't into me. So, where are we going?

MATTHEW: A friend is answering phones at a crisis pregnancy center tonight. I promised to drop by in case she's lonely and maybe pray with her for a few minutes.

ZACK: OK! Now we're talking. There's real life on Christmas Eve! Some chick finds out she's pregnant and totally freaks out! There's the Christmas spirit for you.

MATTHEW: *[smiling]* Actually, that's pretty close to the beginning of the Christmas story. Remember that teen-age, Jewish girl named Mary? She received some pretty shocking news herself.

[Attention shifts to the side stage where MARY and GABRIEL appear as the NARRATOR reads Luke 1:26-38.]

ZACK: So how did Mary break this angel news to her folks?

MATTHEW: Well, I think the hard part was telling her fiancé.

ZACK: I bet he didn't believe her. He dumped her, right?

MATTHEW: Well, that was his first inclination . . .

[Lights go down on the car scene and attention goes to the Bible scene. An angry JOSEPH storms in and lies down to sleep. An angel appears above him as the NARRATOR reads Matthew 1:18-25.]

ZACK: Hey, your friend was all right. I thought she'd be some weird, preachy lady but she was cool. What a drag, though, spending Christmas Eve in an empty crisis center listening to other people's problems. Why's she doing that? Got no life of her own or something?

MATTHEW: She's got a life. Caring for others and reaching out to people who hurt is part of what tonight is all about. Now, I've got to drop off some coats and gloves at my church. It's supper time and I want to help serve the meal.

ZACK: Go right ahead, I'll wait in the car.

MATTHEW: Nice try. I'm sure they've got some work for you.

ZACK: Man, you got a weird way of celebrating the holidays. At least I'll blend in with this gang: a bunch of forgotten people with no place to go on the birthday of some dead guy who's got houses all over the world.

MATTHEW: First of all, Zack, Jesus is very much alive. Second, He actually lived a lot more like these people than you realize. He didn't have a home at first either.

[MARY and JOSEPH enter the side stage to talk to the INNKEEPER who refuses them and sends them to a stable. The NARRATOR reads Luke 2:1-7 as it is being acted out.]

ZACK: All right, we've done the big charity thing and it wasn't too bad. Now, can we just take a break and hang out somewhere with a TV?

MATTHEW: Sure, let's get some coffee.

ZACK: Wow, they're open on Christmas Eve? There's a bummer—having to wait tables tonight. You can't get much Christmas spirit if you're working while the rest of the world is kicking back and drinking eggnog.

MATTHEW: You'd be surprised! On the night Jesus was born a bunch of guys were out doing their job and the Christmas spirit crashed right in on them.

[The SHEPHERDS and ANGELS take the stage while the NARRATOR reads Luke 2:8-20. MATTHEW and ZACK come in again.]

Skits, Plays, and Dramas for Teens and Adults

ZACK: Man, people tell me *I've*
got an answer for everything!
All right, what do you say to
this? These angels said they
had good news for everyone
but Christmas sure isn't for
everyone! Jesus is not for
everyone.

MATTHEW: Are you talking about
anyone in particular?

ZACK: Well, what about Arabs or
Jews or Native Americans?
What about people who are
broke or sick? What about
people who aren't good or
who've messed up their lives?

MATTHEW: That settles it. Come
on. We're going to my church
for the midnight Christmas
service.

*[Car scene is replaced by the
church pew. ZACK looks around
at the congregation for a few
moments.]*

ZACK: I see you got the
"International House of
Jesus" here.

MATTHEW: Jesus really is good
news for people from every
nation, every color, and every
walk of life, Zack.

ZACK: But only good people. I've
still got you there.

MATTHEW: Well, you'll have to
trust me on the details here
but let me assure you that in
this congregation are people

who've made all sorts of wrong choices in life. Sure, some have made good decisions but even *they* are sinners who can't get it right without Jesus. Nobody is here because they deserve to be.

ZACK: Hey, that reminds me of a part of the story you haven't mentioned yet. Didn't those rich dudes bring Jesus gold and stuff?

MATTHEW: I knew you'd remember. That's a part of Christmas that is still happening.

ZACK: What's that?

MATTHEW: Wise men are still seeking Him.

[Church bells ring.]

MATTHEW: It's midnight! Merry Christmas, Zack. Hey, are you OK?

ZACK: I don't know. Seeing all those people clued into God, I feel left out. I just feel like Jesus doesn't even know me. Maybe He forgot about me.

MATTHEW: Do you know what your own name means? *[ZACK shakes his head]* It means "God remembers." God hasn't forgotten you, Zack, and I would love to spend Christmas day telling you more about Him.

ZACK: That's cool about my name, man. What does Matthew mean?

MATTHEW: It means, "gift from God." Merry Christmas, kid.

[Blackout.]

It's Only a Job!

by CAROL S. REDD

Summary: Two treetop angels discuss the ups and downs of their work in this humorous look at the dark side of our Christmas responsibilities.

Characters:

    MELODY—an experienced treetop angel, but ragged around the edges

    GABBY—a mall treetop angel with an obvious nervous twitch

    JOSEPHINE—new treetop angel who wants to bring "peace on earth"

    NARRATOR

Setting: treetop angel break room

Props: Christmas trees with treetop angels on them; cardboard wrapping paper tube; treetop angel costumes—floating, white angel robes, glitter for hair and skin; gummy bears for GABBY's hair

Running Time: 10 minutes

Note: This skit pokes some lighthearted fun at a staff member and family, so be certain this meets the approval of all who are involved.

NARRATOR: Well, Christmastime is here for another year. How is your Christmas season going? Are you and your family filled with wonder and excitement? Are you anticipating being with family and friends? Have you shared God's love and compassion? Or is this season . . . "only a job" . . . that will be over in a week or so? Hmm. "Only a job." . . . Sounds sad, doesn't it? How did that happen? I mean, none of us ever started out thinking of Christmas as "only a job," . . . did we? No, surely not. . . . There was passion and anticipation and joy welling up inside us until we didn't think we could wait any longer to celebrate the birth of Jesus. But somewhere along the way . . .

    This evening *[or morning]* we're going to look at Christmas—not from a human standpoint, but from an angelic standpoint. Oh, not the heavenly ones. But how about, just for fun, of course, we look at Christmas from the standpoint of treetop angels . . . those that are placed on the very top of Christmas trees all over the world. Surely, from their place of honor, as they overlook all that Christmas has to offer, they would never describe Christmas as "only a job" . . . or would they?

[MELODY *enters, brushing her robe, straightening her hair, and looking nervously over her shoulder. She is carrying a cardboard wrapping paper tube. A few seconds later,* GABBY *walks past, occasionally twitching rather violently. She continues twitching occasionally throughout her lines as well as where indicated in the script. She has several gummy bears stuck throughout her hair.]*

MELODY: Gabby? Is that you?

GABBY *[hesitantly]:* Yes . . . I'm Gabby. Why? Who are . . . wait a minute . . . Melody? Is that you?

MELODY: Yes. How are you?

GABBY: Oh, I'm *[gives a violent twitch]* fine. I didn't even recognize you. What in the world happened? You look a little . . . um, messed up.

MELODY: Well, Gabby, you know I've been a treetop angel going on 20 years now . . .

GABBY: Me too! I actually just finished my 18th year and, let me tell you, . . . I'm just about ready to hang it up!

MELODY: Tell me about it. I feel the same way. . . . Matter of fact, I think this is my last year as a treetop angel.

GABBY *[obviously twitching]:* Oh, no. Really?

MELODY: What's wrong with you?

GABBY *[a little defensively]:* What do you mean?

MELODY: You've got that twitching thing going on there. . . . What's that all about?

GABBY: Oh *[demonstrating a twitch]*, that! Well, . . . this year I worked on one of the Christmas trees out at the mall.

MELODY: That doesn't sound so bad.

GABBY: Hmmph. You wouldn't think so. Actually, the job wasn't so bad . . . until . . . until . . . *[starts twitching violently]*

MELODY *[pats her consolingly]:* It's OK. . . . It's OK. . . . Just get a grip . . . and tell me what happened.

GABBY: Bubba happened!

MELODY: What?

GABBY: Bubba . . . and he's not a "what"; he's a "who." He's a little kid that came to the mall every day . . . every day . . . and threw gummy bears at me when his mom wasn't looking. *[twitching]*

MELODY: Oh, yeah, I think I see one. *[reaches out and pulls a gummy bear from* GABBY's *hair]* Hang on a minute.

GABBY: Ouch! *[grabs her head]* Thanks. Anyway, his mom kept screaming *[in a sicky sweet, grating voice],* "Bubba, where are you?" . . . "Bubba, come over here." . . . "Bubba, you'd better get over here before I count to three." But she never . . . NEVER . . . came to get him. He just stayed . . . second after second *[her voice rises in panic after each statement].* . . . minute after minute . . . hour after hour . . . pelting me with those gummy bears. *[frantically looking around]* I think I hear him coming now! *[She tries to hide behind MELODY.]*

MELODY: No, no, Gabby. He's not here. Come on. *[pulls GABBY out from behind her]* You're safe. I promise.

GABBY *[fearfully]*: Are you sure?

MELODY: Positive. *[pats GABBY's hand]* Now settle down.

GABBY: Whew. OK. Let's talk about something else. *[twitching]* Talking about Bubba makes me crazy, . . . what's that you're holding? *[gestures toward cardboard tube]*

MELODY: Well, it used to be attached to my back, . . . you know, to hold me on the tree.

GABBY: Oh, yeah. How come it's not attached anymore? You poor thing. Did you fall off the tree and break?

MELODY: No. . . . I wish it were that simple, . . . but it's a long story. . . .

GABBY: Well, tell me all about it. . . . The more we talk about you, the less time I have to think about Bubba. *[twitches]*

MELODY: Well, . . . OK. But you have to promise not to tell anyone. . . . It's a really weird little story.

GABBY: OK. . . . I promise.

MELODY: Well, up until last year, I used to work on the trees at the mall too. Then I decided I wanted a more "peaceful" job . . . like being an angel on a nice little tree . . . in a nice little house . . . with a nice little family.

GABBY: Well, that sounds pretty . . . "nice" . . . unless you were assigned to Bubba's family!

MELODY: No. . . . Actually, I was assigned to the *[insert last name of preacher]* family.

GABBY: The *[insert last name of preacher]* family? You mean, the preacher's family?

MELODY: That's right. . . .

GABBY: Well, that is great! *[pause]* Or wasn't it?

MELODY: Oh, I thought it would be great too . . . at first . . . but then it turned out to be . . . very unusual.

GABBY: Unusual? Why?

Skits, Plays, and Dramas for Teens and Adults

MELODY: Well, it's just that I thought they would be *[mumbles]*.

GABBY: You thought they would be what?

MELODY: It's just that I thought they would be . . . you know . . .

GABBY: What? You thought they would be what?

MELODY: I thought they would be . . . you know . . . perfect.

GABBY: Perfect?

MELODY: Sure, . . . what with him being the preacher and all . . . and the preacher's wife . . . and the preacher's kids. . . . I just thought they would be . . . perfect.

GABBY: Are you saying they weren't?

MELODY: I'm saying . . . they weren't even close.

GABBY: Not close? Why? What happened?

MELODY: Well, it's just that I was sitting up there on top of their tree . . . minding my own business . . . doing what treetop angels do . . . basically nothing . . . when *[insert name of preacher's wife]* decided that I wasn't sitting quite straight, and I needed to be adjusted.

GABBY: Oh, I hate when that happens.

MELODY: That's not the point. . . . The problem was that she told *[insert preacher's name]* that she couldn't reach me. So she asked him to help her.

GABBY: So? What did he say?

MELODY: He said, "Not now, babe. I'm a little tired. And actually, if you would just fix me a sandwich and a soda, that would be great. Then I think I'll just take a little nap. I'll see if I feel up to helping you fix that angel when I wake up."

GABBY: No!

MELODY: You should have seen the look on her face. . . . It was eerie. . . .

GABBY: What'd she do then?

MELODY: She stomped . . . and I do mean stomped . . . out to the kitchen, . . . slapped together a sandwich, . . . popped the top on a can of soda, . . . stomped back into the living room, and *[insert preacher's name]* was just sitting there staring at the TV. . . . She slammed that stuff down on the coffee table and said, "Don't worry about me, honey. I can fix that angel by myself!"

GABBY: Wow! I didn't think a preacher's wife would ever get mad at her husband.

MELODY: Me neither, . . . but it gets worse.

GABBY: No!

MELODY: Oh, yes. . . . She came back into the living room with a broom

and swatted at me on top of the tree, and I went flying across that room and smashed into the wall!

GABBY: Oh, no! Did *[insert preacher's name]* say anything?

MELODY: Well, when I went flying by he yelled, "Get out of my way. I can't see the TV!"

GABBY: Well, no wonder you grabbed that thing *[gesturing to the tube]* and ran out the door!

MELODY: Well, actually, I didn't leave right then, . . . at least not until . . .

GABBY: Until what?

MELODY: Until *[insert preacher's name]* realized he had made a BIG mistake, so he apologized and they got all mushy. . . . Then *[insert name of preacher's wife]* went to get a glue gun to hot glue this thing to my spine! Have you ever had a tube hot glued to your spine?

GABBY: No!

MELODY: Me neither, . . . and I'm not about to either! That's when I ran for the door and ended up here. *[pause]* What in the world is that?

[JOSEPHINE enters down the center aisle from the back of the church.]

GABBY: I have no idea. . . . But look at her. . . . She sure doesn't look like us.

MELODY: Hey, you. . . . Who are you? You're not by any chance a treetop angel, . . . are you?

JOSEPHINE: Oh, no, . . . but that's my dream. I hope that next year I can get a job as a treetop angel and help to spread peace and love all over the world. *[MELODY and GABBY look at each other questioningly and then stare at JOSEPHINE who is very serious.]* I hope that everyone who looks at me will see my gentle loving spirit. *[begins slowly exiting as she finishes talking]* They will love one another, . . . help one another, . . . reach out to one another . . . all because they have been inspired by me and the love I have for the entire world. . . .

[MELODY and GABBY wait until JOSEPHINE is out of sight and then look at each other and burst out laughing.]

MELODY: Well, what was that all about? Peace to the world? *[laughing]* Who does she think she is—Miss Universe? Whew! That's a good one! Obviously, she's never had anything hot glued to her spine!

[MELODY and GABBY exit up the center aisle as they continue talking.]

GABBY: Right. *[sarcastically]* And everybody is going to love each other to death! Yeah, . . . right. . . . That's a hoot! . . . Wait! *[frantic]* I think I hear Bubba! *[twitching]*

MELODY: No, he's not here. I promise. . . . Oh, wait a minute. . . . *[picking from GABBY's hair]* You've got another gummy bear in your hair.

GABBY: I bet little "Miss Peace to the World" has never been pelted by a giant bag of gummy bears.

MELODY: Right. Little "Miss Everybody Is Just Going to Love One Another" needs to realize that this "Christmas thing" is just another job . . . and nothing else. . . . It's only a job!

GABBY: Exactly! It's only a job!

The Shepherds' Wives

by V. LOUISE CUNNINGHAM

Characters:
>SARAH
>TERAH, young wife
>ELIZABETH, older woman
>MARY
>DEBBIE
>MARCIE
>TAMERA, last minute shopper

Setting: Contemporary scene with a table and chairs, and two Bible-time scenes, one of a kitchen scene and the other a stable. Could use a split stage.

Props: Table, coffeepot, mugs, doll, kettle, blankets, baby clothes

Scene 1

Scene opens on a contemporary setting with three women sitting around a table drinking coffee.

DEBBIE: Hard to believe that Christmas is just around the corner. Do you have everything ready?

TAMERA: Are you kidding? I'm the one who does her shopping on December 24.

MARCIE: I'm finished with everything so I can sit back and enjoy the holidays.

DEBBIE: There always has to be one.

TAMERA: Why couldn't it be me?

MARCIE: Because you have to plan ahead and work on things all year.

TAMERA: I remember my grandmother did that. She hid things in shopping bags all around the house and when the holidays came, she couldn't find the things she had bought.

DEBBIE: At least Mary didn't have to worry about Christmas.

TAMERA: And if you remember, the wise men didn't get there until Jesus was a child. And you think I'm behind on my shopping.

MARCIE: Have you ever thought about the shepherds' wives?

DEBBIE: Do you think the shepherds were married?

TAMERA: Why wouldn't they be? Shepherding would be a job like any other.

MARCIE: I wonder if they sat around like we are now, having a cup of whatever they drank.

Scene 2

A Bible-time scene with Elizabeth sitting at the table.

SARAH *(knocking on door):* Hi, it's just me.

ELIZABETH *(opening door):* Come in. I wondered how long it would be before somebody came to my door.

SARAH: Then your husband told you the same story mine did?

ELIZABETH: I can't say for sure until we compare, but probably.

SARAH: I've never seen Joel so excited. He told me about seeing angels in the sky who told Joel and the other shepherds the Messiah was born. Then the shepherds went to Bethlehem and disturbed some poor couple in a stable to see their baby.

ELIZABETH: Sounds like about the same thing I heard.

SARAH: Do you think there is any truth to it?

(A knock is heard.)

ELIZABETH: It has to be Terah. *(Opens the door.)* Come in Terah. I was just telling Sarah it had to be you.

TERAH: Then your husbands told you the same story?

SARAH: We were just comparing notes. Did Timothy tell you that the sky opened up and it was full of angels?

TERAH: Something like that. Then these beings said the shepherds were to go and find a baby wrapped in swaddling clothes lying in a manger. Doesn't that beat all?

ELIZABETH: You don't think there is truth in that? I wouldn't think that all of the shepherds would dream the same thing on one night.

SARAH: They did find a baby.

TERAH: Yes, but the Messiah wouldn't be born in a stable!

ELIZABETH: Why couldn't He be?

TERAH: I think the Messiah would be born in a palace or at least in the home of nobility, not in a dirty stable.

ELIZABETH: The Messiah is coming for all people. Do you think we would be welcomed into a fancy house to see the Messiah?

TERAH: No, but the Son of God deserves better than to be born in a stable.

ELIZABETH: We have a wonderful God and He does work in mysterious ways.

SARAH: What do you think we should do?

TERAH: About what?

SARAH: Do you think we dare go and see the Messiah?

TERAH: If they are in a stable, they could use some food or blankets. We could take something to them. Do you think that would be all right, Elizabeth?

ELIZABETH: I think that would be a good idea. I have some soup simmering. We could take some of that over.

TERAH: I have some new baby clothes I could take.

ELIZABETH: Are you sure you want to do that?

TERAH: It's all right. By the time I get pregnant again I'll have time to make some more baby things. If He really is the Messiah I would be honored if the mother would accept them.

SARAH: I'll see what I have. Let's meet back here around lunchtime.

TERAH: Sounds good to me.

ELIZABETH: I'll just add a few more vegetables to the soup and I'll be ready in a few minutes. I wonder if the Messiah has really come. I remember when I was a little girl playing with other girls and we'd take turns being the mother of the Messiah. Then when I wasn't chosen I hoped one of our girls would be. I remember hearing that the Messiah was to be born of a virgin. There were a lot of other prophecies, but now my mind goes blank on what they were. It seems like there was one that said where He would be born.

Scene 3

The three women are standing outside the stable. Mary and the baby are inside.

Sarah: Joel said this is the stable. Now that we're here, I'm kind of afraid.

Elizabeth: Why? She can't do more than tell us to go and mind our own business. If she does, you can all come over for soup.

Terah: She'll probably be glad to have some help, since she's a stranger in town.

Sarah: Some people like to be left alone if they aren't feeling well or have just had a baby.

Terah: Maybe they have found a better place to live and they aren't here anymore.

Elizabeth: This soup is getting heavy and we won't find out anything if all we do is stand out here yammering. Let's go in.

Sarah: Now that I think of it, isn't it strange to be carrying some soup into a stable? People might think there's a sick cow in there or something. *(Giggles.)*

Elizabeth: Good morning. Is there anyone here? Hello . . .

Mary: Yes, who is it? I'm over here.

Elizabeth: We heard you gave birth to a son last night and we thought you might like a little lunch brought in.

Mary: That's very kind of you. My husband, Joseph, had to leave for a few minutes, but I'm sure he'll be back soon.

Terah: I brought some baby clothes you might be able to use.

Mary: That's very thoughtful of you. I wasn't able to bring much with us. We were hoping we would be back home before the baby came. We had to be here for the census. When we got here all the inns were full and I was in labor. The innkeeper said we could use his stable.

Terah: What a precious baby. What did you name Him?

Mary: Jesus.

Elizabeth: Of course, it would be. It means the Lord saves.

Mary: Tell me again how you knew I was here.

Sarah: Our husbands are shepherds and they came home all excited. They said the sky opened up and they saw angels. The angels told them they would find you here with a baby and that He was the Messiah.

Mary: Did you believe them?

Terah: I would like to believe.

Mary: If you have a few minutes, I'll tell you and you can make your own decision.

Elizabeth: Are you sure you aren't too tired? We didn't plan on staying very long.

MARY: It won't take very long. I was engaged to Joseph and one night an angel came and told me that I was going to have a baby. I asked how that could be since I had never known a man. The angel replied that the Holy Spirit would come upon me and I would have a child I would call Jesus.

TERAH: Weren't you scared?

MARY: Scared is putting it mildly. I was terrified even though the angel said not to be afraid. When I told Joseph I was pregnant, he was going to divorce me. He didn't understand until an angel came to him.

SARAH: What a relief that must have been.

MARY: It was. I went to visit my cousin Elizabeth, and she was miraculously expecting too. Both she and her husband, Zechariah, are pretty old to be having a baby and an angel spoke to Zechariah in the temple. Because he didn't believe the angel, he was speechless until the baby came.

SARAH: You make it sound so simple. There must have been some difficult times.

MARY: There was the usual tongue wagging when the women in town started counting months and how long Joseph and I had been married.

ELIZABETH: Yes, we women can sometimes be very nasty.

MARY: There were times when I sometimes thought the angel visiting us was a dream and God really didn't talk to me, but last night confirmed again in my mind that this is the Son of God.

SARAH: What was it that reassured you?

MARY: Your husbands coming to see us because angels spoke with them and told them where to find us.

ELIZABETH: That was very strange. Well, Mary, if there isn't anything we can do for you, we will let you rest.

SARAH: Imagine, we saw the Messiah. Thank you, Mary.

Scene 4

This scene is with the three contemporary women sitting at the table.

DEBBIE: You know, in Luke it says that the shepherds told people about the birth and the people who heard it were amazed. I wonder what all those people did after they heard.

MARCIE: I wonder if they believed. After all, you wouldn't think the

Skits, Plays, and Dramas for Teens and Adults

shepherds would be easy people to fool. They were pretty practical.

TAMERA: Isn't it something that God chose hard-working men to be the first witnesses?

MARCIE: Life wasn't easy for the Jews at that time. There were high taxes, they were under Roman law, and a military state was in control. Add to that Greek philosophy and the strict Jewish religion.

DEBBIE: And into that situation God sent His Son.

MARCIE: The amazing thing to me is that although Jesus was a baby, He was God. God was in a manger.

TAMERA: If Jesus had been born in a palace, the simple people would not have been allowed to see Him.

DEBBIE: We can certainly learn from the shepherds.

TAMERA: What's that?

DEBBIE: To go and tell others the good news. The Savior of the world has come and they will want to know Him personally.

TAMERA: Excellent point and I must be going.

MARCIE: To tell others the good news?

TAMERA: That, of course, and to finish my shopping.

How Many Times?

by CAROL S. REDD

Summary: How many times have people rejected God's offer of His most precious gift?

Characters:

GRANDMA	BRANDON
JENNA	LOGAN
MOM	OFFSTAGE VOICE
DAD	

Setting: GRANDMA's house at Christmastime

Set: Christmas tree with wrapped gifts, one very special gift, 3 chairs near the Christmas tree, 2 chairs together at far side of the stage

Props: Christmas tree; wrapped gifts (one of which is a book) for under the tree and some for MOM, DAD, JENNA, BRANDON, and LOGAN to carry in with them; one very special wrapped gift that will not be opened; 5 chairs

Costumes: casual clothing

Running Time: 10 minutes

As drama begins, GRANDMA walks to microphone while holding the one very special gift.

GRANDMA: *[with great enthusiasm]* I can't tell you how exited I am about this gift! Well, actually about Christmas as a whole, but this gift in particular. My granddaughter is just going to be absolutely thrilled when she sees it! She has wanted something like this for the last couple years, and we just weren't able to find it. But last week I was at the mall, just browsing and enjoying the Christmas hustle and bustle, when all of a sudden, there it was! Even better than what she had asked for! It's absolutely the *perfect* gift for her! I can hardly wait until she gets here. I can't wait to see the look on her face when she opens this box! Here, let me just show you ... no, wait ... I'd better not open it. Let's just wait until she gets here. I want you to be just as surprised as she is. It shouldn't be much longer. Thank goodness! I just don't think I can wait any longer.

Skits, Plays, and Dramas for Teens and Adults

[*There's a knock at the door.* GRANDMA *rushes to open it.* MOM, DAD, JENNA, BRANDON, *and* LOGAN *enter and are carrying gifts. All are hugging, calling each other by name, and wishing each other a merry Christmas. They go to the tree and begin exchanging gifts. Adults are seated in chairs and children are sitting on the floor. They all show their excitement and comment on how much they like what they receive. After* JENNA *opens the book from her grandma, she excitedly comments on how much she likes it, then goes to one of the two chairs on the far side of the stage and begins reading. Once everyone is finished opening their gifts,* GRANDMA *picks up the very special gift and walks over to where* JENNA *is seated. The rest of the family stays where they are and quietly interact with one another without talking out loud so that the focus is solely on* JENNA *and* GRANDMA.]

GRANDMA: *[very excited]* Jenna!

JENNA: Yes, Grandma?

GRANDMA: I've got something very special for you!

JENNA: You do?

GRANDMA: Yes, I do and I must tell you that I just can't wait for you to see it! I am so excited about this! *[*GRANDMA *hands the gift to* JENNA, *but* JENNA *doesn't take it.]*

JENNA: Well, would it be OK if I opened it later? I'm kind of busy reading right now.

GRANDMA: *[obviously disappointed]* But, Jenna, I have been waiting all morning for you to get here so I could give this to you. I just know you're going to *love* it! It is the most perfect gift ever!

JENNA: *[takes the box]* It really is pretty, Grandma, but *[putting the gift down]* I think I'll just open it another time. Later today or tonight; sometime when I'm not so busy. *[*JENNA *returns to reading her book.]*

GRANDMA: But, Jenna—

JENNA: Sorry, Grandma, but this book is *really* interesting.

GRANDMA: *[sadly]* But—

[*Everyone freezes in place.*]

OFFSTAGE VOICE: How many times has God offered *His* perfect gift—His precious Son? *[pause]* How many times have people rejected God's gift? *[pause]* How many times have people broken God's heart?

Skits, Plays, and Dramas for Teens and Adults

Jesus: Hope of the Ages

by KAREN L. MECHTLY

Cast:

MATT, modern man

ELIZABETH, woman of Bethlehem

ABIGAIL, woman of Bethlehem

MARTHA, young woman of Bethlehem

CLAUDIUS, Roman soldier

MARCUS, Roman soldier

SIMON, innkeeper

JUDE, tax collector

THOMAS, tax collector

RACHEL, shepherd girl

JACOB, Rachel's grandfather

GABRIEL, angel messenger

CHOIR OF ANGELS

MARY, mother of Jesus (nonspeaking)

JOSEPH, Mary's husband (nonspeaking)

READER

STAGE CREW

SOUND CREW

Act 1

Spotlight on as scene opens on a modern apartment with chair, bookcase, TV, and boom box. Matt enters and throws his coat on the chair.

MATT: It's not fair!! This has been the worst day of my life. I can't believe I was fired. I thought my computer job was secure. My future was so bright. Now I'm a has-been. I've been downsized. *(Pulls ring box out of his pocket, opens it, and looks at it.)* I guess I will take Megan's Christmas present back. Why would she want to marry me now?

(He walks over to his boom box, muttering all the way about life not being fair and turns the box on. "Good Christian Men, Rejoice" is playing. He quickly snaps it off.)

MATT: I don't want to hear that stuff now. What do I have to rejoice about? *(Starts pacing back and forth.)* There are hundreds of people looking for jobs. It will be impossible for me to find one. Computers are the only things I know about and no one needs those workers now. *(Shakes his head.)* And this is supposed to be the season to rejoice. Not me, I have no hope at all. *(Slumps dejectedly on the chair.)* What am I going to do? *(He sighs.)* Maybe there is something on TV. *(Picks up the TV log.)* "Frosty the Snowman" or "It's a Wonderful Life"? I don't think so. *(Throws TV log down and looks around the room.)* I know; I'll read something. *(Walks to bookcase, looks at a few books, then selects a Bible.)* What do you know? Here's the Bible my mom gave me when I left home. She always told me about Jesus when she was alive, but I never listened. And I've never opened this Bible. Maybe she was right. Maybe I can find hope here. *(Opens the Bible.)*

(Lights go out. Matt exits and stage crew removes furniture and puts up Bethlehem background, including an inn and well.)

Act 2

Spotlight on.

CHRISTMAS CHOIR: "O Little Town of Bethlehem"

(Lights on. From right side the three women of Bethlehem enter with their water jars and walk across the stage to the well.)

ELIZABETH *(frowning):* My arms still ache from all the work I did yesterday.

ABIGAIL: Mine too. We work so hard for our husbands and yet they do not appreciate all we do. *(Rubs her back.)*

MARTHA: You would think water ran right into our house the way my family uses it. *(All laugh.)*

ABIGAIL: Has it been hard for you to learn to care for Benjamin and his children?

MARTHA *(nodding her head):* Oh, yes. I thought it would be wonderful to have a husband and children, but I never realized how hard wives have to work. Every day it is the same thing—carry water, keep the fire going, bake bread, feed the little ones, mend their clothes.

ABIGAIL: Well, you better get used to it. That's what you will be doing for the rest of your life.

ELIZABETH: You are not more than a child yourself. *(Pats Martha's stomach.)* And probably soon you will have a little one of your own.

MARTHA *(trying to smile):* I know little ones are a gift from God, so I would welcome another one to care for. *(Pauses, then says excitedly.)* Perhaps God will choose me to be the mother of the Messiah. My grandfather told me He would be born here in Bethlehem.

ABIGAIL: Ha! You do not believe those old tales about God sending a Savior, do you?

MARTHA *(puzzled):* Of course I do. My grandfather told me about the Messiah every night at bedtime. The holy Scriptures tell how He will come from Heaven and make our lives better. There will be no more hard work . . .

ELIZABETH *(interrupting):* Some of us think the ancient writers made that story up to give the people something to look forward to.

ABIGAIL: Yes, that story was meant to comfort our people during the captivity in Babylon. It was a hard time for them. But it is only a story.

MARTHA: No, it's not just a story! My grandfather said God himself helped the ancient men write the Scriptures. They wrote the truth. They did not make up stories. God *will* send His Messiah.

ELIZABETH: You can look forward to a Messiah if you want to. But I'm not going to waste my time. People have been looking for a Savior for hundreds of years and he has not yet come.

ABIGAIL: You will change your mind when you grow older. The holy Scriptures are beautiful to listen to, but they do not apply to us today.

(Elizabeth and Abigail fill their jars in the well and turn to leave.)

ELIZABETH: Dreamer. You will wise up.

(Elizabeth and Abigail leave the way they came.)

MARTHA *(fills her jar from the well then looks up to Heaven):* Oh God, I do believe You will send a Messiah to save us. I am looking forward to that wonderful day.

(Lights out. Martha pushes well to side as she exits.)

Act 3

(Spotlight on.)

CHRISTMAS CHOIR: "Come, Thou Long-Expected Jesus"

(Lights up. Roman soldiers and tax collectors enter stage noisily. They stop in front of an inn.)

MARCUS: It sure is crowded tonight in Bethlehem. I hope we can find a room in an inn.

CLAUDIUS: Let's try this one. Maybe it is not yet filled. *(Knocks on door.)*

SIMON *(opening the door):* Do you need a room, Sir?

CLAUDIUS: Yes we do.

SIMON *(looking at all four):* I am sorry, but tonight I can only accommodate two more travelers. As long as I have had this inn I have never had so many people knock on my door in one evening.

MARCUS *(to tax collectors as he motions them on):* You men move on and find rooms for yourselves. Claudius and I will stay here.

JUDE: Why you? We are just as important as you in this registering and taxing process. And besides, we are Jews. You are Romans. Move aside and let us go in.

MARCUS: I will not. You might be Jews, but we know the people hate you as much as they hate us. Now, go.

THOMAS *(folds his arms and says defiantly):* We are not moving. There might not be another room available tonight. As the innkeeper has said, this town is full of travelers tonight.

CLAUDIUS *(sneering):* Maybe you will have to sleep on the ground. Of course you are too *soft* to be able to do that.

THOMAS: You miserable Roman. *(He lunges toward Claudius.)*

CLAUDIUS *(draws his sword and puts it on Thomas' chest):* Get out of here, you scum, or you will not see the sun rise tomorrow.

JUDE *(pulls Thomas away):* Thomas, do not be foolish. We can find another inn. You cannot fight a Roman soldier and win.

(Jude and Thomas walk a few paces away.)

CLAUDIUS (laughs wickedly): I knew they would see it my way.

MARCUS (to Innkeeper): Now, about that room . . .

(Claudius puts sword to Simon's chest.)

MARCUS: It better be the best room you have and the charges better be fair.

(Claudius puts sword away.)

SIMON (shaking): Y-y-yes, Sir. Right this way.

(Simon, Claudius, and Marcus walk through inn door.)

JUDE: Thomas, what were you thinking? You could have been killed.

THOMAS: I know. But it angers me that the Romans have taken over our land. Even though I am working for Rome, I cannot stand the Romans.

JUDE: I agree. But what can we do?

THOMAS: We can look for the promised Messiah. He will be a mighty soldier. When He comes, we will have victory over the Romans.

JUDE: Do you really think God cares about us any more? He has allowed our country to be taken over by foreigners. We are no longer free. We are all scared.

THOMAS: He does care for us. We are His chosen people and He will rescue us. I know He will.

(Lights out. Thomas and Jude leave. Stage crew replaces Bethlehem scenery with hillside scenery, can include a small fake fire.)

Act 4

Spotlight on.

CHRISTMAS CHOIR: "While Shepherds Watched Their Flocks"

(Lights on. Shepherd girl Rachel, a stuffed lamb by her side, and her grandfather, Jacob, are sitting around a small fire. Sheep baa in the background.)

JACOB: Rachel, look at the night sky. The stars are brighter than I have ever seen them before.

RACHEL: They are beautiful tonight, Grandfather. *(She sighs.)*

JACOB: Is something bothering you, my granddaughter?

(Rachel nods her head.)

JACOB: You can tell me about it.

RACHEL: When I went into Bethlehem today to get some cheese and bread from home, a group of boys laughed at me. They made fun of my old cloak and they said I smelled bad, like sheep.

JACOB: People have always made fun of us shepherds, even though we do an important job by guarding the sheep.

RACHEL: They chased me all the way home. They were going to throw stones at me, but I ducked inside the door just in time.

JACOB: Next time they start to tease you, remind them our great King David was a shepherd boy and our patriarch Isaac and Jacob had wives who were shepherd girls, just like you.

RACHEL: I was too scared to say anything. *(Pause.)* Grandfather, please tell me about the Messiah again.

JACOB: Of course, Rachel. Our holy Scriptures tell us that God will send His Son. He will be called Wonderful Counselor, Mighty God, Everlasting Father and the Prince of Peace. He will reign on David's throne.

RACHEL: Does that mean the Messiah will like shepherds, Grandfather?

JACOB: Oh, yes! The Messiah will love all the people of the earth, rich or poor—important or not. In fact, our Scriptures say the Messiah will care for His people as a shepherd cares for his sheep.

RACHEL *(picks up little stuffed lamb)*: That's comforting. *(Pause.)* Do you think God will send the Messiah while we are alive?

JACOB: I hope so, but I do not know. I have been looking for him my whole lifetime. Now I am getting old and . . .

(Gabriel enters with spotlight on him. Lights out. Jacob and Rachel fall prostrate on the ground.)

GABRIEL: "Do not be afraid. I bring you good news of great joy that will be for all the people. Today in the town of David a Savior has been born to you; he is Christ the Lord. This will be a sign to you: You will find a baby wrapped in cloths and lying in a manger" (Luke 2:10-12).

Skits, Plays, and Dramas for Teens and Adults

(Spotlight on.)

ANGEL CHOIR: "Angels We Have Heard on High"

(Angels exit. Spotlight goes off. Lights back on.)

RACHEL: Were those real angels, Grandfather, or was I dreaming?
JACOB: They were real! Imagine, God sent His angels to announce the
  Messiah's birth to poor shepherds.
RACHEL: Let us hurry to Bethlehem and find Him.

*(Jacob and Rachel rush off. Lights off. Mary, Joseph, and manger are set
up on center stage.)*

Act 5

(Spotlight on.)

CHRISTMAS CHOIR: "Adoration" and "O Come, All Ye Faithful"

(Lights on manger scene. Jacob and Rachel rush in.)

JACOB: Praise God! I am blessed to see the Messiah with my own eyes.
RACHEL: Praise God! The Prince of Peace has come.

(They kneel at the manger.)

READER: "But you, Bethlehem Ephrathah, though you are small among
  the clans of Judah, out of you will come for me one who will be ruler
  over Israel, whose origins are from of old, from ancient times. He will
  stand and shepherd his flock in the strength of the Lord, in the majesty
  of the name of the Lord his God. And they will live securely, for then
  his greatness will reach to the ends of the earth. And he will be their
  peace" (Micah 5:2, 4, 5).
THOMAS *(entering):* Praise God! I knew He would not forget His
  people. *(He kneels at the manger.)*
READER: "'The days are coming,' declares the Lord, 'when I will
  fulfill the gracious promise I made to the house of Israel and to the

house of Judah. In those days and at that time I will make a righteous Branch sprout from David's line; he will do what is just and right in the land. In those days Judah will be saved and Jerusalem will live in safety. This is the name by which it will be called: The Lord Our Righteousness'" (Jeremiah 33:14-16).

MARTHA: Praise God! I knew it was true. God has sent a Savior. *(She kneels at the manger.)*

READER: "'She will give birth to a son, and you are to give him the name Jesus, because he will save his people from their sins.' All this took place to fulfill what the Lord had said through the prophet: 'The virgin will be with child and will give birth to a son, and they will call him Immanuel'—which means, 'God with us'" (Matthew 1:21-23).

MATT: Praise God! He gives us hope by sending us His Son. *(He kneels at the manger.)*

READER: "Here is my servant, whom I uphold, my chosen one in whom I delight; I will put my Spirit on him and he will bring justice to the nations. In faithfulness he will bring forth justice; he will not falter or be discouraged till he establishes justice on earth. In his law the islands will put their hope" (Isaiah 42:1, 3, 4).

CONGREGATION OR CHOIR: "Joy to the World!"

A Dish of Blessings

by DIANNE McINTOSH

Summary: Audrey and Ralph's grown children are not coming home for Christmas. Audrey is heartbroken so Ralph takes matters into his own hands and invites a socially-mixed group of loners and losers over for Christmas. When the big day arrives, the party gets out of hand but is saved from total disaster through focusing on the birth of Jesus and what it really means to all of us, no matter where we sit socially.

Characters

AUDREY, the wife

RALPH, the husband

EILEEN, Audrey's friend

ANCHOR, a homeless man, should be able to sing

TONY, a homeless man

MR. WHIPPETS, well-dressed, distinguished-looking older man

MRS. WHIPPETS, his wife

ALICE, a lonely newcomer to town

HOLLY, Alice's daughter

ERIC, Alice's son

Setting and props: Living room scene with sofa, easy chairs, lamps, end tables, piano, Christmas decorations, newspaper, two phones (one of which is off to the side with a chair for EILEEN), cookies, foam cups, gifts, wrapping paper, bows, extra chairs, poinsettia, Bible, hand-held video game, portable radio with headphones

Lights up on living room scene. AUDREY *is talking on the phone.* RALPH *is sitting in an easy chair reading the newspaper.*

AUDREY: Of course, we understand, April. But Ethan can't make it either, so that means no family here for Christmas. It'll be so lonely, just your dad and I. Think of it, just the two of us opening our pathetic little presents and eating a pathetic little frozen turkey dinner . . . watching football. *(She pauses while April talks.* RALPH *lowers the newspaper and tilts his head; you can see he is thinking.)* Well, no, I could cook, but what fun is it to cook a nice dinner when there's no one here to share it with? I cook for your father every day. *(Pause)* I know I don't have to watch football either, but think how your father will feel watching football on Christmas all by himself—it's heartbreaking. (RALPH *rolls his eyes.)* All right then, April, we'll see you on New Year's Eve. *(Pause)* Yes, yes, it'll be fun. *(Pause)* I do understand. OK, bye now. (AUDREY *dabs her eyes.)*

RALPH *(looking out from behind his paper):* So April can't make it either?

AUDREY: That's right. It's just you and I. Isn't it terrible?

RALPH: Just you and I . . . it doesn't sound that bad.

AUDREY: Well, it is. And I vote we just cancel Christmas.

RALPH: Oh, Audrey, we can still have Christmas. Maybe we can do something extra special this year.

AUDREY *(her face lighting up a little):* Like what Ralph?

RALPH: Maybe I'll surprise you.

(Lights go out. RALPH *leaves. Lights come up on* AUDREY *and* EILEEN. AUDREY *is talking on the phone to* EILEEN *who is off to the side.)*

EILEEN: Anyway, we're so excited. All the kids will be here for Christmas, and this is our first holiday with a grandbaby. I just can't believe how good God is to us.

AUDREY *(sarcastically):* Yes, God is really dishing out the blessings this year.

EILEEN: Why, Audrey! You don't sound like you mean it.

AUDREY: It's just that none of our kids is coming home for Christmas.

EILEEN: I'm so sorry, Audrey. I didn't know. And you so love the holidays.

AUDREY: It's OK. In fact, Ralph says we're going to do something extra special. So I am getting a little excited about that. Maybe he's taking me to some fancy restaurant or maybe a getaway to Hawaii. I hope it is something really special.

EILEEN: I'm sure it will be great. I have to go. I promised Lydia I'd take her Christmas shopping. We have so much fun together.

AUDREY *(sighing):* Daughters are a real blessing. Have fun, Eileen.

EILEEN: Merry Christmas!

AUDREY *(flatly):* Yeah, Merry Christmas.

(Lights go out, then come up full in living room. AUDREY *is wrapping a present. She slaps a bow on top.)*

AUDREY (*saying the words, not singing*): Deck the halls with boughs of holly. Fa-la-la-la-la-la-la-la-la. We wish you a Merry Christmas.

(AUDREY *takes the gift and tosses it under the tree.* RALPH *comes in whistling. He is obviously excited about something. She looks up.*)

AUDREY: Well, what are you so chipper about?

RALPH: Christmas is only two days away, and I'm happy. Plus, I have put together a wonderful Christmas surprise for you.

AUDREY: Really? Can you tell me?

RALPH: Well, I think I'd better tell you, since you'll have to do most of the preparation.

AUDREY: Preparation? Ralph, this doesn't sound like fun to me.

RALPH: It's all how you look at it, . . . I think. . . . Anyway, I stopped by the church and talked with the minister about what we could do to make Christmas special this year. He suggested . . .

AUDREY: Church! The minister! What were you thinking? OK, tell me. Just go ahead and tell me.

RALPH: I'm trying to, Audrey. He suggested that we invite people over who don't have family or anyone to spend Christmas with. So I looked around and I have quite a list of folks who are really excited to come and share Christmas with us.

AUDREY: Stop! Tell me you haven't already invited them.

RALPH: Now, Audrey, don't get hysterical. I thought it would take some of the pressure off you if I went ahead and did the inviting; you know, one less thing for you to do.

AUDREY: How many?

RALPH: Seven.

AUDREY: Who?

RALPH: Let's see—Mr. and Mrs. Whippets.

AUDREY: Well, they're OK, a little stuffy. . . . Who else?

RALPH: Anchor and Tony.

AUDREY: What! They live under the bridge! How did you get in touch with them? How could you invite the Whippets and then Anchor and Tony? That's like having chocolate on tuna fish!

RALPH: Now, Audrey, my criteria wasn't whether people went together. It was who needed a place to spend Christmas. Anchor and Tony are very nice, and you should have seen how thrilled they were to get invited. It was really touching.

AUDREY *(between gritted teeth):* OK, Ralph, that's four. Who are the other three?

RALPH: Well, this is the exciting part. I was at the grocery store, and I overheard a woman talking with her kids about how they were going to do their best to have a nice Christmas even though they would be alone. It turns out they just moved here, and they don't know anyone, and they didn't look like they had much.

AUDREY *(interrupting, starts slow and even, her voice rising as she talks until she is yelling):* So let me get this straight. You went up to total strangers and invited them to our home to spend the most wonderful day of the year?

RALPH: Audrey, Honey, this is a real opportunity for us to minister. These people all need God's love. What a wonderful way to share it, by inviting them to come to our home on the most joyous day of the year. Can't you see God's hand in this?

AUDREY: Oh, yes, I do see God's hand. He's really dishing out the blessings this year, isn't He?

(Lights go out, then come up on AUDREY *and* EILEEN. AUDREY *is on the sofa and talking on the phone with* EILEEN *again.)*

AUDREY: So that's my big special surprise from Ralph. My Christmas is ruined. I can't even imagine how I'm going to handle it—the Whippets, Anchor and Tony, and then this woman with two kids. I don't even know their names!

EILEEN: Now, Audrey, maybe Ralph is right. Maybe this is a great opportunity to minister. God works in mysterious ways.

AUDREY: Oh, I know that. The worst part is that I feel so guilty because I'm so upset. But, Eileen, it's *Christmas.* You know—family, presents, Christmas trees, mistletoe, eggnog. It all adds up to Christmas.

EILEEN: But that really isn't it at all.

AUDREY: What do you mean?

EILEEN: Christmas is really the birth of Jesus. God's great gift to mankind. The rest is just traditions that we love. I confess I love them too, but they don't make Christmas. Giving the gift of Jesus does.

AUDREY *(pauses and sighs):* Well, Eileen, you have a good point. I hate to admit it. I'm still mad at Ralph. He's getting a lump of coal in his stocking this year—but maybe I can try to give a little to this odd group my husband has invited.

Skits, Plays, and Dramas for Teens and Adults

EILEEN: That a girl. I'll pray for you. Lydia and I are baking Christmas cookies all afternoon so I'll bring you over a couple of plates of them. I gotta go. Chin up!

AUDREY: Right, chin up and I best get busy too. Bye.

(Lights go out. AUDREY *and* EILEEN *exit. Lights come up on living room. Living room is decorated and ready for guests. Extra chairs are put out.* RALPH *is wearing a new tie and nibbling on cookies. [SFX: Doorbell rings]* AUDREY *shouts from offstage.)*

AUDREY: Can you get the door, Ralph? I'm just finishing up in the kitchen.

RALPH: Yes, Dear.

*(*RALPH *walks to door and opens it. The Whippets are standing on the threshold. They are a well-dressed older couple, very distinguished looking.)*

RALPH: Merry Christmas!

MR. WHIPPETS: Merry Christmas, Ralph. So good of you to invite us. Here is a little token of our appreciation. *(He hands* RALPH *a potted poinsettia.)*

RALPH: Well, thank you very much, Mr. Whippets. Come in. May I take your coats?

MRS. WHIPPETS: Yes, thank you. This snow is so lovely. *(Looks at* MR. WHIPPETS.*)* Perfect Christmas weather, isn't it, Dear? Really perfect.

MR. WHIPPETS: Yes, Dear, perfect.

(There is an uncomfortable pause.)

RALPH: So . . . ah . . . have a seat. Have some cookies. May I get you some eggnog or hot apple cider?

MRS. WHIPPETS: That would be lovely. I believe I'd prefer the cider *(Looks at* MR. WHIPPETS*)*, wouldn't you, Dear? Doesn't that sound just perfect for today?

MR. WHIPPETS: Yes, Dear, I think you are absolutely right. I believe I will also have the hot apple cider. Very good, yes.

*(*RALPH *leaves to get the cider. [SFX: doorbell rings.] The Whippets sit. [SFX: doorbell rings again, over and over; ding dong, ding dong. It*

continues, sounding more and more frantic until RALPH *opens the door.]*
The Whippets raise their eyebrows. RALPH *returns with the cider. The cider*
is in foam holiday cups. MRS. WHIPPETS *takes a cup, raises her eyebrows,*
and looks a little put out. ANCHOR *and* TONY *are banging on the door and*
shouting.)

ANCHOR: Hey, hey, . . . hello, is anybody home or what?

*(*RALPH *goes to door and opens it.* ANCHOR *and* TONY *are standing there in*
dirty, layered clothing. Their hair is messy but they look like they tried to
clean up.)

RALPH: Merry Christmas. I'm sorry. I was out of earshot for a minute.
ANCHOR: That's OK. I was starting to think you might not have meant
    it—the invite I mean.
TONY: Yeah. It's cold out here. May we come in?
RALPH: Of course, of course, I'm sorry. Come in. *(*ANCHOR *and* TONY *enter*
    and look around as if they are in a really ritzy place. They look at each
    other and smile.) Anchor, Tony, this is Mr. and Mrs. Whippets.
ANCHOR: Real honor and all that. *(*ANCHOR *smiles and then turns to* RALPH.*)*
    May we have some cider?
TONY: Yeah. It's cold out there.

*(*MR. *and* MRS. WHIPPETS *are frozen and staring.)*

RALPH: Cider, yes. I'll just go get it. Help yourselves to some cookies. May
    I take your coats?
ANCHOR: No! No, we never give up our coats.

*(*RALPH *exits.* ANCHOR *and* TONY *dig into the cookies, putting a few in their*
pockets. There is an uncomfortable silence. MR. *and* MRS. WHIPPETS *look*
slightly frightened. MRS. WHIPPETS *pulls her purse in close to her.)*

MRS. WHIPPETS: Lovely weather, don't you think—for Christmas, I mean?
TONY: Yeah, lovely. Freezing cold with snow and a blizzard coming. Real
    nice, lady.

(SFX: Doorbell rings, gentle knock. ANCHOR *goes to answer. Standing*
outside is ALICE *with her two children,* HOLLY *and* ERIC.*)*

Skits, Plays, and Dramas for Teens and Adults

Anchor: Yeah, Merry Christmas. You coming in or what?

Alice: Oh, we must have the wrong house. We're looking for Ralph and Audrey Finstand.

(Ralph comes in with the cider, hands it off to Tony, and then rushes to the door.)

Ralph: Alice, I'm so glad you could make it.

Alice: Well, we are too. The children are so excited to be here.

(Children look bored. They push past Ralph. Holly runs over to the cookie table and starts shoving cookies in her mouth. Eric sits on a chair and starts playing a hand-held video game. He is listening to music on headphones and ignores everyone.)

Ralph: Well, help yourself to some cookies. . . . Would you like some cider?

Alice: No, thank you. Holly, put those cookies down this instant.

Holly: I'm hungry. You said we'd eat good here.

Alice: Holly, please be quiet.

(Tony takes cookie plate and offers Eric a cookie. Eric looks at him like "drop dead" and takes a stick of gum out of his pocket, unwraps it, and begins chewing gum. He adjusts his headphone. Tony shrugs, takes a cookie, puts the tray down, and tips his hat at Mrs. Whippets. Holly makes a loud noise and begins playing with fragile trinkets on the tree. Mr. and Mrs. Whippets lean forward and look sternly and worriedly at Holly and Alice. Anchor and Tony are not too interested in Holly. Finally, Alice pulls the items away from Holly. Mrs. Whippets leans back and turns to where Anchor is next to her. Anchor has inched his way over to her and is sitting right next to her smiling as she turns. Mrs. Whippets jumps. Anchor reaches out and touches her cookie.)

Anchor: Lady, are you gonna eat that?

(She slowly, with shock, hands it over to him. Anchor takes the cookie but does it by touching her whole hand. Mrs. Whippets holds her hand out to Mr. Whippets, who seems flustered. He brushes it off, shrugging with a "what can I do?" expression. Anchor smiles, eats with his mouth

open, coughs and a little cookie flies out. MRS. WHIPPETS *brushes herself off.* TONY *takes out a vile looking handkerchief, blows his nose, takes off his hat, wipes his head with the handkerchief, then stuffs it back in his pocket.* TONY *then proceeds to wipe his nose one last time with the back of his hand. He tops it all off with taking a cookie off the tray, looking it over, and then putting it back.* TONY *picks up another cookie and starts to eat it, notices the horror on* MR. *and* MRS. WHIPPETS *faces and attempts to pass the cookie tray to them.)*

MRS. WHIPPETS *(very firm and with feeling):* No. Thank you.

*(*MR. WHIPPETS *has a frozen but fading smile on his face.* MRS. WHIPPETS *looks at him and mouths, "Do something!"* HOLLY *sneaks over to where* RALPH *is sitting and shouts in his ear.)*

HOLLY: When do we eat, mister?
RALPH: That's a good question. I'll go ask Audrey how things are going. I'll be right back.

*(*AUDREY *enters from other door carrying a tray.* RALPH *rushes over to her.)*

RALPH: Audrey, do something. You were right. This mix of people isn't working. Things are going crazy.
AUDREY: I thought the point of this was to share Jesus' love with people.
RALPH: Yes?
AUDREY: So what have you shared with them so far?
RALPH: Cider. Oh, and cookies.
AUDREY: Well, I guess we need to add a little bit of true Christmas.

*(*AUDREY *unloads her tray and turns to the group. She looks at* ALICE *and* HOLLY.*)*

AUDREY: You must be Alice. I'm glad to meet you. And this is . . .
ALICE: Holly and my son, Eric.
AUDREY: Thank you for coming. *(Turns to* MRS. WHIPPETS.*)* Mrs. Whippets?
MRS. WHIPPETS: Yes, Dear?
AUDREY: I remember that you used to play the piano for church. Do you think you could play some carols for us?
MRS. WHIPPETS: Well, I don't know. I haven't, I mean . . . well . . . *(She acts*

flustered, looks at MR. WHIPPETS. *He nods his head in encouragement.*
MRS. WHIPPETS *takes one last look at* ANCHOR.*)* Yes, I'd love to.

*(*MRS. WHIPPETS *goes to piano and starts playing "Silent Night."* ANCHOR
*starts singing and has a very nice voice. They all stop what they are doing
and listen. Song ends.)*

MR. WHIPPETS: Well, sir, you have a fine voice. We need a voice like yours
in our church choir.

ANCHOR: I used to sing in a choir, a long time ago.

TONY: Yeah. Me too. When I was a kid I loved Christmas.

ALICE: I used to love Christmas too. Now it just seems like so much work.

HOLLY: I love Christmas. I love presents and Santa Claus and candy and
presents and bright lights and presents.

ALICE: Enough Holly, we get the point.

AUDREY: You know what Holly? I thought that was all Christmas was too,
and I'm grown up. I should know better. A friend of mine reminded
me that Christmas is really God's gift to us. It starts right here in
your heart.

HOLLY: In my heart?

AUDREY: That's right. It's Jesus' birthday, but the best gift we can give
Him is our hearts. The funny thing is that it turns out to be the
greatest gift we will ever receive.

HOLLY: So the gift we give is the gift we get. Sounds weird. How much
does it cost?

AUDREY: That's the best part. It's free. Do you know the story of Jesus?

HOLLY: No. I've heard of Him, but I don't pay attention to His story 'cause
Santa Claus is more fun.

AUDREY: Ralph, will you read the story of Jesus' birth?

RALPH: Yes, what a good idea. I'll get my Bible and . . . *(he is looking it up)*
here we are *(reads about Jesus' birth from Luke).*

(As he reads, project art of scenes of the birth of Jesus.)

RALPH: "In the sixth month, God sent the angel Gabriel to Nazareth, a
town in Galilee, to a virgin pledged to be married to a man named
Joseph, a descendent of David. The virgin's name was Mary. The
angel went to her and said, 'Greetings, you who are highly favored!
The Lord is with you.'

"Mary was greatly troubled at his words and wondered what kind of greeting this might be. But the angel said to her, 'Do not be afraid, Mary, you have found favor with God. You will be with child and give birth to a son, and you are to give him the name Jesus. He will be great and will be called the Son of the Most High. The Lord God will give him the throne of his father David, and he will reign over the house of Jacob forever; his kingdom will never end.'

"'How will this be,' Mary asked the angel, 'since I am a virgin?'

"The angel answered, 'The Holy Spirit will come upon you, and the power of the Most High will overshadow you. So the holy one to be born will be called the Son of God. Even Elizabeth your relative is going to have a child in her old age, and she who was said to be barren is in her sixth month. For nothing is impossible with God.'

"'I am the Lord's servant,' Mary answered. 'May it be to me as you have said.' Then the angel left her" (Luke 1:26-38).

"In those days Caesar Augustus issued a decree that a census should be taken of the entire Roman world. (This was the first census that took place while Quirinius was governor of Syria.) And everyone went to his own town to register.

"So Joseph also went up from the town of Nazareth in Galilee to Judea, to Bethlehem the town of David, because he belonged to the house and line of David. He went there to register with Mary, who was pledged to be married to him and was expecting a child. While they were there, the time came for the baby to be born, and she gave birth to her firstborn, a son. She wrapped him in cloths and placed him in a manger, because there was no room for them in the inn.

"And there were shepherds living out in the fields nearby, keeping watch over their flocks at night. An angel of the Lord appeared to them, and the glory of the Lord shone around them, and they were terrified. But the angel said to them, 'Do not be afraid. I bring you good news of great joy that will be for all the people. Today in the town of David a Savior has been born to you; he is Christ the Lord. This will be a sign to you: You will find a baby wrapped in cloths and lying in a manger.'

"Suddenly a great company of heavenly host appeared with the angel praising God and saying, 'Glory to God in the highest, and on earth peace to men on whom his favor rests.' When the angels had left them and gone into heaven, the shepherds said to one another, 'Let's go to Bethlehem and see this thing that has happened, which the Lord has told us about.'

Skits, Plays, and Dramas for Teens and Adults

"So they hurried off and found Mary and Joseph, and the baby, who was lying in a manger. When they had seen him, they spread the word concerning what had been told them about this child, and all who heard it were amazed at what the shepherds said to them. But Mary treasured up all these things and pondered them in her heart. The shepherds returned, glorifying and praising God for all the things they had heard and seen, which were just as they had been told" (Luke 2:1-20).

(There is silence as everyone absorbs the story.)

ALICE: The promised Messiah, how wonderful. It sounds like a fairy tale. I haven't heard it read in years.

MR. WHIPPETS: I don't think I've heard it in years either—I mean really heard it. God is truly amazing.

MRS. WHIPPETS: Amazing.

RALPH: Yes, He is. And He's real, Alice. Look at us here today. We're all so different and yet He loves each one of us just the same.

(ANCHOR and TONY look at each other, then at the others.)

ANCHOR AND TONY: Us too?

AUDREY: You too.

HOLLY: I like God. He sounds better than Santa Claus.

ALICE *(laughing):* Oh, Holly!

MRS. WHIPPETS: Shall we sing some more?

MR. WHIPPETS: Yes, Dear, we shall sing.

(Everyone moves around the piano. They sing the first verse of "Joy to the World," "Hark! the Herald Angels Sing," and "We Wish You a Merry Christmas." Lights go out. Everyone leaves except RALPH and AUDREY. Lights come up on RALPH and AUDREY sitting in the living room looking exhausted.)

RALPH: Well, Audrey, I have to hand it to you. You really pulled it off.

AUDREY: It was nice, wasn't it?

RALPH: Could you believe Mr. and Mrs. Whippets offering Anchor and Tony the spare room over their garage?

AUDREY: Well, they do have to shovel snow. *(Chuckles, then pause)* Ralph, this was an extra special Christmas. For the first time in years, my heart felt full of the greatest Gift. The Gift I ignore and sometimes take for granted. But this year, right now, I feel Jesus, and I can say with complete joy "Merry Christmas." God really did dish out the blessings this year.

(Blackout)

The Lamb Is Born

by V. LOUISE CUNNINGHAM

Characters

ABBY, friend	JOSEPH
BETH, writer	JOHN
JUNIAS, shepherd	JEW 1
RUFUS, shepherd	JEW 2
ANGEL 1	JEW 3
GROUP OF ANGELS	CROWD
MARY	

Props: a ceramic lamb, Christmas decorations (all related to the biblical accounts of Christ's birth), table, chairs, coffeepot, mugs, paper, pencil, large lamb cutouts, shepherd crooks, manger, coat, purse, spotlight. Have small paper lambs on hand so people can write down the "gifts" they are bringing.

Costumes: modern and Bible-times clothes

Setting: Two ladies discuss lambs throughout the Bible and their significance. The staging of the Bible scenes can be simple or a big production. The ladies can be seated in front of the stage or off to the side, and lights come on them when they speak.

Scene 1

Two friends are visiting. There is a ceramic lamb and a variety of Christmas decorations on the table.

ABBY: What on earth are you doing with all your Christmas things out? Did I fall asleep for a couple of months?

BETH: I know it is early, but I'm trying to get an idea so I can write the Christmas play for church. It seems like we have used every idea possible and I just can't come up with a new idea.

ABBY: And all this mess isn't helping? *(Picks up the ceramic lamb.)* I've always wondered why you put this lamb out at Christmas and Easter.

BETH *(thinking for a few seconds):* That's it! The Lamb is born. That's the title. Thank you. Thank you.

ABBY: Glad I could help. What did I do?

BETH: Don't you see? Jesus was born, and He was called the Lamb of God.

ABBY: And of course the night that Jesus was born, it was the shepherds the angels told about the newborn Messiah.

BETH: There's speculation that the shepherds were watching the flock of sheep that were used for sacrifices at the temple in Jerusalem.

ABBY: And how fitting is that? Jesus was our sacrifice.

BETH: I can see how the Christmas skit can all come together. We can use cardboard cutouts of sheep on the stage, and they are surrounding the shepherds. Then there is a bright light, and the shepherds fall down on their knees and shield their eyes.

Scene 2

SHEPHERDS *are on their knees with their arms covering their faces from the bright light. One by one the* SHEPHERDS *dare to lift their eyes to look at the* ANGELS.

ANGEL 1: "Do not be afraid. I bring you good news of great joy that will be for all the people. Today in the town of David a Savior has been born to you; he is Christ the Lord. This will be a sign to you: You will find a baby wrapped in cloths and lying in a manger" (Luke 2:10-12).

ANGEL CHORUS: "Glory to God in the highest, and on earth peace to men on whom his favor rests" (Luke 2:14).

(Congregation can sing "Angels, from the Realms of Glory," "Angels We Have Heard on High," or "Hark! the Herald Angels Sing." Dim lights on ANGELS. *The* SHEPHERDS *look at each other.)*

RUFUS: You did see what I saw, didn't you—the bright light and an angel talking to us?

JUNIAS: Boy, am I glad that you saw it too. I thought I was hallucinating.

RUFUS: So what are we waiting for? Let's go to Bethlehem.

JUNIAS: I'm glad that the angel gave us an idea of what to look for.

RUFUS: I don't suppose that there have been that many babies born tonight.

JUNIAS: This one will be in a manger, so that narrows it down.

Scene 3

Nativity scene with Joseph, Mary, *baby, and manger. The* Shepherds *arrive and kneel in worship while little children and the congregation sing.*

CHILDREN: "Away in a Manger"

CONGREGATION: "O Little Town of Bethlehem"

Scene 4

Lights back on the ladies as they are sipping their coffee.

ABBY: So at least you have a pretty good opening with the angels. The congregation gets involved by singing, and then, of course, everyone enjoys hearing the little children sing—they are so precious! What are you going to do next?

BETH: Well, I said we could work with the lamb. *(Picks up the ceramic lamb.)* The next time I can think of where a lamb is involved is at the baptism of Jesus.

ABBY: So I suppose you are going to stage a river.

BETH: No, but we can try to make people think there is a river on stage. The emphasis isn't going to be on water but on John the Baptist and what he said.

Scene 5

Crowd scene. Dialog taken from John 1:19-31.

JOHN: "I am not the Christ."

JEW 1: "Then who are you? Are you Elijah?"

JOHN: "I am not."

JEW 2: "Are you the Prophet?"

JOHN: "No."

JEW 3: "Who are you? Give us an answer to take back to those who sent us. What do you say about yourself?"

JOHN: "I am the voice of one calling in the desert, 'Make straight the way for the Lord.'"

JEW 1: "Why then do you baptize if you are not the Christ, nor Elijah, nor the Prophet?"

JOHN: "I baptize with water, but among you stands one you do not know. He is the one who comes after me, the thongs of whose sandals I am not worthy to untie. . . . Look *(JOHN points offstage)*, the Lamb of God, who takes away the sin of the world! This is the one I meant when I said, 'A man who comes after me has surpassed me because he was before me. I myself did not know him, but the reason I came baptizing with water was that he might be revealed to Israel.'"

Scene 6

Back to the ladies at the table.

BETH: Then I need to decide whether I should have two disciples continue on where Andrew finds Peter and tells him about Jesus.

ABBY: This doesn't seem like much of a Christmas play.

BETH: My outlook is that Christmas wouldn't make any difference if there wasn't an Easter.

ABBY: That is certainly true. So do you include a Christmas focus when you write about the crucifixion of Jesus?

BETH: No, not really.

ABBY: So there really isn't much mention of lambs and sacrifices until the time of the last supper when the disciples were getting ready for the

Passover. You could go into how the Passover began with the Israelites getting ready to leave Egypt. Each family was to prepare a lamb.

BETH: I don't know if I want to go back too much into the history of the Passover. But I do have to show the significance of Jesus' being considered the Passover Lamb.

ABBY: Somewhere you could have one of your characters say something about the people taking the blood from the lamb and putting it on the doorposts so that the Lord would pass over without claiming the life of the firstborn.

BETH: I am just bogged down when I get to the ending. How can I get back to the Christmas story?

ABBY (picking up the lamb): Maybe you could set the play at a gift store, and a customer could come in and pick up the lamb. It could be wearing a red and green ribbon.

BETH: Or maybe we could go back to the scene of the shepherds bowing at the manger and . . .

ABBY: And the congregation could come forward row by row and lay down gifts at the nativity scene. We could provide a basket—or another manger.

BETH: OK, that might work if the people are told about it in advance so that they come prepared with gifts. It could be nonperishable food that could be given to people who need it. But it would be nice if there could be some sort of dedication of themselves.

ABBY: OK, how about giving out paper lambs so people could write down a Christmas "gift" they could bring to the Savior? It could all fit, since as believers we are called sheep in the Bible and Jesus is our Shepherd.

BETH: That might work. We could put suggestions in the program bulletin so everyone could get an idea. The "gifts" would need to be things that are meaningful, such as the gift of obedience—with a note of an area where it is hard to obey.

ABBY: The gift of forgiveness would mean they would try to make amends to those they need to forgive.

BETH: We could include that we will give a gift of our time to the Lord to spend more time with Him. And, of course, no one would be expected to sign his or her name. . . . I think this might work.

ABBY: It might take a lot of time for all the people to come forward row by row. What are the rest of the people supposed to do?

BETH: That could be an opportunity for the choir to sing some of the special music they have prepared, mixed with Christmas carols that the congregation could sing. Yes, this will all work. *(Starts tapping a pencil.)*

ABBY: So that is my cue to leave so you can start writing it all down.

BETH: Oh, no, have another cup of coffee.

ABBY: That's okay. I need to get some errands finished anyway, and I don't want to stop the productivity of a creative genius at work. See you later. *(Gathers up her coat and purse and leaves.)*

(BETH begins to write as lights fade. Manger scene is lighted and the minister or worship leader invites people to come forward with their "gifts" for the King. Music may proceed as the director wishes.)

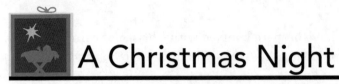

A Christmas Night

by ROBIN M. MONTGOMERY

Time: 45 minutes–1 hour

"The Wise Man" (page 171), "The Innkeeper" (page 172), "Shepherd's Night" (page 173), and "Mary's Letter" (page 174) may all be performed as one longer service. Or each may stand alone and be performed separately. A suggested service outline follows if all four skits are used. You may wish to substitute familiar songs of your own in place of the suggested songs.

Narrator: Isaiah 9:2: "The people walking in darkness have seen a great light; on those living in the land of the shadow of death a light has dawned."

Skit: "The Wise Man"

Song: "O Little Town of Bethlehem"

Narrator: John 1:10: "He was in the world, and though the world was made through him, the world did not recognize him."

Skit: "The Innkeeper"

Song: "Silent Night"

Narrator: John 1:14: "We have seen his glory, the glory of the One and Only, who came from the Father, full of grace and truth."

Skit: "Shepherd's Night"

Song: "O Come, All Ye Faithful"

Narrator: Luke 1:38: "'I am the Lord's servant,' Mary answered. 'May

Skits, Plays, and Dramas for Teens and Adults

it be to me as you have said."' Luke 2:19: "But Mary treasured up all these things and pondered them in her heart."

Skit: "Mary's Letter"

Song [to be played or sung solo as spotlight shines on Mary]: "Mary, Did You Know?"

THE WISE MAN

Summary: A wise man first sees the star of Bethlehem and wonders at its significance.
Characters:
  Wise man
  Servant
Setting: outdoors/palace roof in Bible times
Props: rich robe for wise man, simple robe for servant, scroll
Running Time: 5 minutes

The Wise man *stands gazing into the sky.*

Wise man [*to himself*]: I have studied the stars since I was but a youth—and never before have I seen anything like it. Nowhere in the prophecies of Persia is there mention of a star such as this.

[*The* Servant *enters stage with scroll in hand.*]

Servant: My lord.
Wise man [*turns and faces* servant]: Have you the scroll?
Servant: Yes, my lord. [*hands the scroll to him*] From the writings of the Hebrews, as you requested.
Wise man: Thank you. You may go.

[*Servant bows and exits.* Wise man *unrolls the scroll and fingers the words.*]

WISE MAN: See how ancient are the words. Perhaps the answer to the star lies somewhere in these Hebrew writings. *[reads from the scroll]* The people living in darkness have seen a great light. On those living in the shadow of death, a light has dawned.

[He looks up, and his gaze is pulled to the heavens.]

WISE MAN: What are you, Great Light, that alters the constellations? Why do you stir my soul like no other star before you? What great moment do you speak of? *[lifts hands to the sky]* Oh, Great God of the Hebrews, show me the meaning of the star.

THE INNKEEPER

Summary: A busy innkeeper with a full inn sends a young couple to the stable.
Characters:
INNKEEPER'S WIFE
INNKEEPER
Setting: cozy room with a fireplace in a Bethlehem inn
Props: fireplace; bench or mat next to fire for innkeeper's wife; small wooden table and bench for innkeeper; cloth, needle, and thread for innkeeper's wife's sewing; parchment-looking paper and quill for innkeeper's accounts; lamp
Running Time: 5 minutes

The INNKEEPER'S WIFE is seated by the fire quietly working on some sewing. There is the sound of a door closing offstage. The INNKEEPER enters.

INNKEEPER'S WIFE: Someone else wants a room, eh? At this hour, no less.
INNKEEPER *[sets the lamp on the desk, and seats himself to begin tallying again on his very satisfactory accounts]*: Uh-huh.
INNKEEPER'S WIFE: Census stragglers, no doubt. Or worse yet, Roman soldiers!
INNKEEPER: Humph! No, no one *that* important.
INNKEEPER'S WIFE: Ha!
INNKEEPER: Just a young couple from Nazareth. His wife is pregnant. She looks huge! As you did at nine months—remember?

INNKEEPER'S WIFE: I wish I could forget! Such a miserable time I had too. Ah, well, it's too bad they didn't arrive this afternoon. With the rooms being full since supper, we've had to turn away at least a dozen more just this evening.

INNKEEPER: I told them they could use our stable. Unless you think we should give them our bed with her being pregnant and all. . . .

INNKEEPER'S WIFE *[concentrates on picking out a missed stitch]:* I'm sure they won't be too picky at this hour. Besides, it's not as if they're someone *important!* Come now, dear, finish tallying up those accounts. I'm tired!

INNKEEPER: Yes, dear. *[picks up his quill and looks down at his accounts, and then pauses thoughtfully]* So why do I feel as if *I'm* the one missing something? *[shrugs his shoulders and bends his head to his accounts]*

SHEPHERD'S NIGHT

Summary: Two shepherds discuss their encounter with angels.
Characters:
OBED—a shepherd of Bethlehem
JACOB—a shepherd of Bethlehem
Setting: field outside Bethlehem, immediately following the angels' appearance
Props: simple robes and staffs for the shepherds, sheep [optional]
Running Time: 5 minutes

OBED *[rubbing his eyes]:* Did you just see what I saw?

JACOB *[trembling]:* Angels. Angels everywhere!

OBED: That's what I saw, but I can hardly believe it.

JACOB: I wouldn't believe it either if I hadn't just seen it with my own eyes.

OBED: And heard it too. Such music! *[holds hands up to the sky]* Such beautiful music! I wish it could have gone on forever. . . .

JACOB: And did you hear what the angel said? The Christ child has been born.

OBED *[grabs JACOB by the shoulders and shakes him]:* Do you realize what this means? The Savior—our Messiah—is here! In Bethlehem. Right here! *[paces back and forth]* Didn't the angel say we could find Him wrapped in cloths and lying in a manger?

JACOB: Yes . . . but . . . do you think *we're* supposed to go find Him?

OBED: That's exactly what I mean.

JACOB: But we're just shepherds . . . and He is . . . the Messiah!

OBED *[stops pacing]:* Jacob! We just had an invitation from Heaven! What more do you need? *[shakes head]* Why the angels chose to tell *us*, I have no idea. But if what the angel said is true, then I want to see Him with my own eyes. *[turns as if to go, then pauses, and looks back]* Are you coming?

JACOB: Yes. Yes. You're right, Obed. I'll go with you.

OBED *[shouts and lifts hands in air]:* The Savior has been born!

JACOB: Glory to God in the highest!

[Both shepherds hurry offstage.]

MARY'S LETTER

Summary: Mary writes a letter to her cousin Elizabeth, following the birth of Mary's baby, Jesus.

Characters:
    MARY—nonspeaking part
    ZECHARIAH—nonspeaking part
    ELIZABETH—nonspeaking part
    MARY'S VOICE
    NARRATOR

Setting: the stable, the morning following Jesus' birth; Zechariah and Elizabeth's home

Props: feeding box with hay, doll wrapped in blanket for baby Jesus, doll wrapped in blanket for baby John, 2 pieces of parchment for the letters, a quill for Mary to write with, simple Bible costumes for all characters

Note: Baby John was about 6 months old at the time of Jesus' birth. If you have a baby and his parents who could play the parts of Zechariah, Elizabeth, and John, it would add to the reality of the scene.

Running Time: 5 minutes

Stage left, MARY is sitting and writing her letter. Jesus is asleep in the manger nearby.

Stage right, ELIZABETH and ZECHARIAH are reading the letter as they take turns holding baby John.

The NARRATOR'S voice and MARY'S voice come from the speaker. Spotlight shifts from MARY—as she writes the letter—to ELIZABETH as she reads it.

NARRATOR: History teaches us that Mary, the mother of Jesus, was probably an uneducated girl who couldn't read or write. But if she were able to, how would she describe Jesus' birth in a letter to her cousin Elizabeth?

MARY'S VOICE *[slowly and thoughtfully as though writing the letter as she speaks it]:*

Dearest Elizabeth,

My heart overflows with such gladness and joy! I fear that I will burst if I do not write you—you who believed from the beginning. He is here at last!

That first hour, we could not keep our eyes off of Him. Joseph named Him Jesus, just as the angel told him to. And after Joseph had spoken His name, Joseph held our tiny baby in his arms and wept. I heard him whisper, "So this is what God looks like."

Then, even before the morning light began to dawn, shepherds crowded softly around Jesus and began to worship Him! There was awe in their voices as they told of the angel's announcement on the hillside: "Today in the town of David a Savior has been born to you; he is Christ the Lord [Luke 2:11]." They told how the sky burst into song as a great company of angels sang glory to God! Then, as quickly as they came, they left—not returning to their flocks, but to tell others!

Oh, Elizabeth, I cannot even begin to describe the joy that filled my heart as I heard the shepherds repeat the angel's announcement. They echoed the angel's promise to me, "He will be great and will be called the Son of the Most High. The Lord God will give him the throne of his father David, and he will reign over the house of Jacob forever. His kingdom will never end [Luke 1:32, 33]." Such a promise! When I look at Jesus, wrapped in nothing but simple cloths, laid in a crude manger, that promise seems impossible—but I know that with our God, nothing is impossible!

I try to imagine what Jesus' life will be like. I see His tiny eyes half closed and I wonder—when He looks at the world around Him, the sea, the sky, the land—will He remember creating it all? Will He look at people and see right into their hearts? I hold His little feet in the palm of my hand—feet so much like any other baby's—yet I am awed by the thought that these feet have walked the very streets of Heaven. How long until they are covered with the dust of this earth? Where will they take Him? His hands are so tiny—yet how strong is His grip! Will they hold a carpenter's hammer and chisel, like Joseph's hands? How many lives will be healed through His touch? And His heart, His tiny heart that has beat since before time began—how many times will it be broken over the mess we have made of our world?

I do not know. Perhaps it is best that way. All I know is that His promises are true. "A Savior has been born. . . ." And He is right here among us!

Praise His Mighty Name, for He has made the impossible possible!

I am the Lord's servant,
Mary

It Should Bring Joy
a Christmas Meditation

by STACY POPEJOY

The *celebration* of Christmas has for many of us become somewhat incidental to the *preparation* for Christmas. With all the shopping, concerts, plays, parties, family gatherings, cooking, decorating, corresponding, and wrapping—in addition to the normal routines of each day—time and energy have been stretched to all human limits. That which God had intended to be a joyous and uplifting event has become a season of tiring and burdensome activity that most people can't wait to put behind them. People's attempts to create joy often result in overwhelming anxiety and emptiness. There is little time, and much worse, little desire, to celebrate. This cannot be the way God intended for us to acknowledge the anniversary of the birth of His Son and His gift to us.

"I bring you good news of great joy . . ." These were the words of the angel to the shepherds on that quiet night. This message was intended to bring joy, and it did. God had presented the world with a wonderful gift. A Savior. A Shepherd. A King. All that the people had needed and prayed for and waited for had finally come to them. For these people, peace, light, hope, and life were now freely available. What good news that was. This gift of love—God's only Son—was right there with them, in the flesh. Immanuel. Jesus. The very definition of great joy! Thus, the first Christmas celebration began!

The shepherds made no plans for an elaborate party. No special notices of their pilgrimage were sent out. They didn't bother with fancy clothes or to prepare a royal feast. They just went. They hurried off to see the things that were told to them. They went to give honor to the one who was born to bring joy back to their empty hearts. They went to offer those empty hearts to Him, the Son of God, their Savior, as an act of worship and celebration.

As well, wise men from the East traveled to see Him who was born to bring joy to the world. These men, though rich, happy, and fulfilled by the world's standards, came to honor and worship Jesus because they believed that the true king, the true fulfillment, and true source of joy was given by God in the gift of that little baby. Though they came bearing costly gifts to *give*, they came knowing they would truly *receive* that which is priceless. Oh, what great joy!

Each year at Christmas, people send themselves into financial, emotional, and physical depression trying to bring into their lives, and the lives of others, the feeling of joy that Christmas promises. But the joy of Christmas is not a feeling. It cannot be purchased, created, decorated, or wrapped. There is no program or accomplishment that will activate it in a person's heart. The joy of Christmas is embodied in the child Himself. *Jesus Christ*, God's free gift to people, is the great joy promised by the angel. Only by seeking Jesus and sharing Him with others will each man, woman, and child find the true joy of Christmas.

So beginning this Christmas, let us stop focusing so much time and energy on preparations that will only leave us void of the joy we desire. Instead, let us return our energies to seeking and celebrating the child who has guaranteed joy—our great joy—Jesus Christ!

The Search for Christmas

by CAROL S. REDD

Summary: Two women search for Christmas in very different places.

Characters:

> CAITLIN—a woman who is shopping, wrapping, and decorating in her search for Christmas
>
> VAL—a woman who finds Christmas at the local nativity scene; also a vocalist
>
> MARY—nonspeaking part, part of nativity scene
>
> JOSEPH—nonspeaking part, part of nativity scene
>
> JESUS—nonspeaking part; part of nativity scene; a doll wrapped in a blanket could be used

Setting: on a city street, beside a community or church nativity scene

Props: Bible costumes for Mary and Joseph; manger and hay for stable; Christmas outfit with bells for Caitlin; full shopping bags

Running Time: 10 minutes

[MARY, JOSEPH, and JESUS are stage left. VAL enters stage right. CAITLIN loudly sings "Jingle Bells" as she enters down the center aisle dressed in a Christmas outfit that jingles as she walks and carries several full shopping bags. She sees VAL at the front and calls to her.]

CAITLIN: Val! How are you? It's been so long!

VAL: Caitlin? Is that you? . . . I don't think I've seen you since Jackie's party. . . . That was almost two years ago. And look at you! You look like . . . like . . .

CAITLIN: Christmas?

VAL: Well, yeah, . . . I guess. . . . How come you look like that?

CAITLIN: It's because I'm on a Christmas mission.

VAL: A Christmas mission?

CAITLIN: That's right. . . . I'm meeting up with some friends, and we're going out to "search for Christmas."

VAL: Search for Christmas?

CAITLIN: Right. . . . We're going to shop. . . . Well, *[indicating her bags]*

shop some MORE. We're going to eat (a LOT), and then we're going back to my house to put up my Christmas tree and wrap packages. If we don't have the Christmas spirit by the time this night is over, I don't think we'll EVER have it. Hey, . . . why don't you go with us?

[VAL is busy looking at the nativity and doesn't respond.]

CAITLIN: Hello! Val?

VAL: Oh, I'm sorry. . . . What did you say?

CAITLIN: I was just saying that my friends and I are going out to "find" Christmas. . . . Do you want to go with us? Val? Hello! Val, . . . what are you looking at?

VAL: Oh, . . . sorry. . . . I was just looking at that . . . what's going on over there . . . where those people are. . . . See them?

CAITLIN: Oh, that. . . . It's nothing.

VAL: Nothing?

CAITLIN: Well, it's just a nativity scene. . . . It's nothing really. They do it every year. . . . No big deal. So what do you say? Want to go with us on our big "Christmas search"?

[VAL continues looking between the nativity and CAITLIN.]

CAITLIN [continues]: Come on. . . . It'll be fun. And besides, I even have the car tonight. . . . I'm ready to party. What do you say?

VAL: Well, . . .

CAITLIN: We're going to find Christmas, . . . remember?

VAL: Well [hesitantly], . . . maybe I will.

CAITLIN: Great! Let's go!

VAL: Well, you go on ahead. . . . I'll catch up with you in a minute.

CAITLIN: Fine. . . . I'll go get the car and meet you at the corner. . . . Don't take long though. . . . I want to get started.

[CAITLIN exits down the center aisle. VAL hesitantly and thoughtfully walks to the nativity, sits in front of the manger, and sings "Away in a Manger" or another appropriate song. When the song is finished, CAITLIN reenters down the center aisle.]

CAITLIN: Come on, Val! I'm getting tired of waiting! What's taking you so long?

[VAL gets up from her seat in front of the nativity and walks forward to talk to CAITLIN.]

VAL: You know, Caitlin, . . . I think I'm going to pass on your offer. . . . Maybe we can get together another time.

CAITLIN: But, Val, we were going to "search for Christmas," . . . remember?

VAL: I know. That's OK. . . . You go ahead . . . and, anyway [looking back at nativity], . . . I think I've already found it.

[Bring stage lights down and exit.]

Shopping with Molly

by MARGARET PRIMROSE

Summary: A couple discovers the spirit of giving when they take a young girl to the mall to purchase gifts.

Characters:

TERRI DAVIS—organizer of program to provide gifts for children in need

DON MILLER—slightly goofy guy, sponsor of Molly

SUSAN MILLER—Don's wife and sponsor of Molly

MOLLY—an 8-year-old girl

NARRATOR—speaks one line at the end of the skit

Setting: Scene One—church office; Scene Two—bench in a mall

Props: Scene One—desk and 3 chairs for church office; index card and pen; Scene Two—bench; bag of chocolate chip cookies; shopping bag with gifts: a teddy bear, Barbie of Swan Lake® doll (or another popular doll), a CD of a Christian group your kids like, women's bath and body gift set; gift bags for each gift

Running Time: 15 minutes

SCENE ONE

TERRI is sitting at her desk working when DON and SUSAN MILLER enter.

TERRI: Oh, hi, Don and Susan. You must be here to pick up your shopping partner.

DON: Yes, we are. Sorry we're a few minutes late. The car engine doesn't like this cold weather!

TERRI: Let's see. . . . *[consults a card on her desk]* You'll be taking Molly with you today. She and a few of the other kids are playing in the children's church room while they wait. Do you know Molly?

SUSAN: No, not yet. But our daughter goes to school with her brother John, so we know a little bit about her family.

TERRI: Yes. *[consults her card]* She has a baby brother, Micah, a younger sister, Alana, and her older brother is John. Their mom works so hard to keep things together. This will be a great treat for Molly!

SUSAN: Hey, it's a treat for us. Now that our kids are older, we miss shopping for the younger ones. This will be great fun, won't it, honey? *[She nudges her husband.]*

DON: You're just excited that we're going shopping!

TERRI *[winks at Susan]:* Oh, I can understand that. Now do you two have any other questions?

DON *[looks at his wife for confirmation, and she shakes her head no]:* No, I think we're ready to go.

TERRI: All right, then. I just need you to sign this card so that I know where you're going to shop and approximately how long you'll be gone. We'd like to have your cell phone number too, just in case we need to get ahold of you. And while you fill all that in, I'll go get Molly.

[TERRI exits. SUSAN works on filling out the card while DON paces and rubs his hands nervously.]

DON: Well, this'll be a first for us. I sure hope we know what we're doing!

SUSAN: Don't worry, dear. I've got it under control.

[TERRI returns with MOLLY.]

TERRI: Molly, this is Don and Susan Miller, who are going to take you Christmas shopping today.

DON *[in a high voice]:* Hi, Molly, I'm Susan. *[MOLLY giggles.]* What? I don't look like a Susan to you?

SUSAN *[good-naturedly smacks her husband's arm]:* Don, stop it! Don't pay any attention to him, Molly. We are very glad to meet you. I hope you're ready to hit the mall!

MOLLY: Yes, I am. Thank you.

SUSAN *[holds out her hand to MOLLY who takes it]:* Then let's us ladies take off! *[over her shoulder to DON]* We'll let you tag along too, Don!

DON: What a relief! We'll see you later, Terri. Thanks so much for putting all this together.

TERRI: You're welcome. See you in a while.

[All exit. Lights are cut.]

Scene Two

Don, Susan, and Molly enter. Don is carrying shopping bags full of gifts. The empty gift bags should also be in the shopping bags. Susan is holding the bag of chocolate chip cookies. There is a bench in the middle of the stage.

Susan: Whew! I'm tired from all this walking. How about you, Molly?

Molly: Yes, a little.

Susan: Here's a bench. Let's sit down and have a cookie. *[Susan and Molly sit on the bench. Don places the shopping bags on the floor in front of the bench.]* Do you like chocolate chip?

Molly: They're my favorite!

Susan: Mine too! *[She hands a cookie to Molly and takes one for herself.]* Do you want one, Don?

Don: Nope. Those three chili dogs I had earlier will hold me.

Susan: Chili dogs over chocolate! What is the world coming to? . . . Hey, Molly, while we're sitting here, why don't we go over the gifts we have, and see what we still need to find?

Molly: OK.

[Susan and Molly continue nibbling on their cookies while Don pulls each gift out of the bags.]

Don: That's a great idea! Let's see what we have here. *[He reaches into the bag and, with a flourish, pulls each item out.]* First, a teddy bear . . . for? *[He looks questioningly at Molly.]*

Molly: Baby Micah.

Susan: He'll love that, Molly!

[Don sets the teddy on the bench next to Molly. If he feels comfortable doing it, he can move the teddy bear around and make it talk—"Yes, he will, Molly!"—and give Molly hugs.]

Don: And next, ladies and gentlemen, we have a . . . *[He pulls the doll from the shopping bag and questioningly waves it in front of the ladies.]*

Susan and Molly *[together]*: Barbie of Swan Lake® doll! *[or whatever doll you have chosen]*

Don *[sets the doll next to the teddy bear]*: I knew that.

MOLLY: That's for Alana.

SUSAN: Your little sister, right? The doll is beautiful—what a great gift-giver you are!

DON: The next item we have is . . . a *[name of group]* CD.

MOLLY: My brother listens to music all the time, so I hope he likes it.

SUSAN: Yep. Our daughter has that CD. John will love their music.

DON: And finally, finally, the last item we have is a . . . a . . . bunch of bath-type lotion stuff.

MOLLY: It smells pretty!

SUSAN: Trust me, Molly, your mom works so hard taking care of you guys. She'll love having some pretty stuff for herself.

DON: Now, Molly, we're missing something really important here! Do you have any idea what it is?

[MOLLY shyly shakes her head no.]

SUSAN: There's nothing here for you! What would you like to have? We could get a doll for you, or a new outfit, or what about a new watch? *[MOLLY shyly shakes her head no each time an item is mentioned.]*

MOLLY: No, thank you. I can't think of anything. I just wanted to get stuff for my family so that I would have presents to give them for Christmas.

DON: Molly, that is great! That's what Christmas is all about. I know it makes you feel so happy to give gifts to your family.

SUSAN: Hey, I know what we can do. Let's get out the gift bags and put your presents in them. That way they'll be all ready for when you get home.

DON: And then there's more shopping to do. You see, Susan and I want to get that happy, giving feeling too. And that means that we want to give something to you!

SUSAN: You know what? I think Jesus is very happy with you, Molly. You've figured out what Christmas is about!

[Lights go out; then NARRATOR reads.]

NARRATOR: You'll not likely go wrong here if you keep remembering that "The Lord Jesus himself said: 'It is more blessed to give than to receive'" [Acts 20:35, *NIV*].

The Rich Kid's Birthday

by JOHN COSPER

Summary: A couple that only attends church at Christmas begins to contemplate their eternal fate and starts to wonder about their faith.

Characters:
>   BECKY and DONALD—married couple, holiday church attenders
>   CAROLINE—friend of Becky
>   HURLEY—coworker of Donald

Setting: church lobby

Props: none

Costumes: shirt and tie for DONALD, dress for BECKY, casual for the rest

Running Time: 5 minutes

BECKY and DONALD enter. BECKY is in a nice winter dress appropriate for church. DONALD is in a shirt and tie, which he is adjusting. BECKY looks at him.

BECKY: Remove that tie again, and I'll break your fingers.

DONALD: I don't want to wear a tie!

BECKY: This is the only time we go to church, outside of Easter. There's no reason not to look nice.

DONALD: Other than the fact that every other guy in here is NOT wearing a tie?

BECKY: Will you stop? You sound like a child.

DONALD: I feel like a child. This is just like when I was ten years old and Mom made me go to Hermie Williams's birthday party.

BECKY: Who?

DONALD: The rich kid in the neighborhood. He was a total jerk. Nobody liked him, but all our parents made us go because he was the rich kid.

BECKY: This isn't Hermie Williams's birthday. It's our Lord and Savior's, so straighten up and look holy!

[CAROLINE walks across.]

CAROLINE: Well, hello, Becky!
BECKY: Caroline, how are you?

[CAROLINE exits.]

BECKY: Did you see that? Caroline Springfield thinks we're good
    Christians.
DONALD: Like I care what Caroline Springfield thinks of me.
BECKY: You'll care when she tells her husband what a good man you are
    and he invites you to golf at Barrington.
DONALD: Touche.
BECKY: Well, where shall we sit? Top balcony, back row?
DONALD: Uh-uh! Lower level, back row.
BECKY: No balcony?
DONALD: Too much of a chance we'll get caught in stair traffic. Then we'll
    never get into the restaurant.
BECKY: Fine, lower level it is.

[HURLEY enters.]

HURLEY: Donald? Wow! I didn't know you went here!
DONALD: Hey, Hurley.
HURLEY: Wow, praise the Lord, there's another believer at work. How
    come you never told me?
DONALD: Oh, you know me—walk, not talk. Or something like that.
HURLEY: That is so deep. You know we have a men's prayer group that
    meets weekly, don't you?
DONALD: Of course I do!
HURLEY: Really? I've never seen you there.
DONALD: Well, I meant to go, but no one ever got me signed up.
HURLEY: How 'bout we do that now? C'mon, I'll walk you over.
DONALD: You know, Hurley, it's Christmas Sunday, and I'd like to spend it
    with the family. But how about next Sunday we get me all signed up?
HURLEY: Fantastic, pal! Meet you right here?
DONALD: Right here next week.
HURLEY: Outta sight!

[HURLEY exits. DONALD takes a deep breath.]

Skits, Plays, and Dramas for Teens and Adults

DONALD: Did you see that? That guy almost had me going to a prayer group. This church is getting too dangerous.

BECKY: You're right. Maybe we should do a different church next year.

DONALD: Are you nuts?

BECKY: If no one knows you, you won't get the nosy prayer group invites.

DONALD: No, but we will stick out. As soon as they see us, they'll start to stare 'cause they'll KNOW.

BECKY: Know what?

DONALD: Know we're headed for hell.

[BECKY is taken aback.]

BECKY: I didn't know you felt that way.

DONALD: I . . . I didn't mean it that way.

BECKY: Sure sounded like it. It just popped right out.

DONALD: Well, I didn't mean it.

BECKY: Are you sure?

DONALD: Of course I'm sure.

BECKY: Because I've never felt like I might not be a . . .

DONALD: What?

BECKY: A Christian.

DONALD: Well, it's not like we walk the walk every day of our lives. We don't pray. Don't read the Bible. Don't go to church except on holidays. Honestly, I don't see why we even go then. If God is all that Christians make Him out to be, He knows we're faking it. So why bother?

BECKY: Because . . . what if we need God one day? We want Him to know who we are. You know, in case we need Him.

DONALD: So what are we going to do about it?

BECKY: Maybe it's time to do more than just show up at Christmas.

DONALD: You don't want me to go to that prayer group, do you?

BECKY: I was thinking we could start by listening.

DONALD: Listening?

BECKY: For the first time in my life, I want to hear what the preacher has to say.

DONALD: I can do that. What do you think we'll learn?

BECKY: I don't know. But there's gotta be something these people who come every week know that I don't. Whatever it is, I'd sure like to find out.

[Blackout.]

Christmas Idol

by JOHN COSPER

Summary: A reality show gives three judges a chance to pick who is the ultimate Christmas idol.

Characters:

RYAN—the incredibly cheesy host of the show, should be a young man

ANDY—a middle-aged man who thinks he is a rapper, contest judge

DARLA—a middle-aged woman who is nice to everyone but doesn't like SILAS, contest judge

SILAS—a middle-aged man with a British accent, thinks very highly of himself, rude to most people, contest judge

FROSTY THE SNOWMAN

RUDOLPH

SANTA

SCROOGE

THE THREE KINGS—three men, nonspeaking roles

Setting: TV studio

Props: table, microphone, bright orange hunting cap

Costumes: modern-day clothing including a sparkly and obnoxious shirt for DARLA, tight black T-shirt for SILAS, oversized button-down shirt for ANDY, suit for RYAN, reindeer costume, SANTA costume, suit for SCROOGE, FROSTY THE SNOWMAN costume, Bible-times costumes for the THREE KINGS

Theme music plays. Lights up. RYAN is at center. The judges are seated at a table stage right.

RYAN: Welcome back to *Christmas Idol*. I'm Ryan Cheesefest. This holiday season, our judges went around the world looking for the individual that most represents the holiday season.

[FROSTY enters.]

FROSTY: Hi, I'm Frosty the Snowman. I'm so Christmassy, I'm made out of snow! I've got a corncob pipe, a button nose, and I'm just the jolliest guy you'd ever meet.

RYAN: Well, you sure look jolly. Judges, what do you say?

DARLA: Aw, Frosty, you're so cute. You're the perfect winter weather friend.

ANDY: Yo, yo, dog, check this out. I've never seen someone like you. You're full of snow. This is true.

RYAN: And how about you, Silas?

SILAS: Frosty? Bah, humbug!

DARLA: Oh come on, Silas! He's so cute, and he's made of snow. Plus, his fashion is excellent. That scarf and hat combination is incredible!

SILAS: Am I the only one who remembers that it's Christmas in the south too? He'd melt away on Miami Beach. He's a pathetic excuse for a Christmas idol. Get out of here!

[FROSTY frowns and exits.]

RYAN: Sorry, Frosty. Better luck next time. Who is our next contestant? He's furry! He's friendly!

[RUDOLPH enters].

RUDOLPH: Hi there, folks! I'm Rudolph the red-nosed reindeer and I love Christmas! I love it so much that when I think of it, my nose lights up all red and bright!

DARLA: Aww, Rudolph, that's so cute! I love it. And red *is* in this season!

RUDOLPH: Thanks, Darla. I think you're cute too!

ANDY: Yo, yo, yo, dog!

RUDOLPH: I'm not a dog. I'm a reindeer.

ANDY: Yo, you call yourself a reindeer? I call you full of Christmas cheer.

RYAN: How about it, Silas?

SILAS: Are you daft? You know, the problem here is the holiday season coincides with hunting season. We send him out, he's liable to get shot.

DARLA: Who would shoot a sweet deer like him?

SILAS: *[puts on a hunting cap]* Me, for one. Nothing like venison for Christmas dinner.

[RUDOLPH screams and runs offstage.]

DARLA: I can't believe you're such a jerk! Eating deer?

SILAS: What do you think I brought to last year's potluck dinner?

DARLA: You said it was pheasant!

RYAN: OK, folks, let's move right along. Our next contestant hails from the North Pole.

[SANTA enters.]

SANTA: Ho, ho, ho! Merry Christmas!

DARLA: Santa! It's Santa!

ANDY: Ho, ho, ho and hee, hee, hee, Santa, yo, he's da man for me!

RYAN: Sounds like we have a winner. Silas?

SILAS: Let's see. He's old. He frightens small children. Is that what we are looking for?

DARLA: Silas! I can't believe you're saying this about Santa.

SILAS: I can't believe no one's said it before!

ANDY: Silas, you the lowest thug! Why you gotta say humbug?

SILAS: I only speak the truth. Santa, hit the gym!

SANTA: Looks like someone wants to be on the naughty list again!

SILAS: Oh wow, I'm shaking in my stockings. Get lost.

[SANTA exits.]

DARLA: Jerk.

RYAN: Let's see if our next contestant can fare any better. Welcome from jolly old England, Ebenezer Scrooge.

[SCROOGE enters.]

RYAN: Merry Christmas, Mr. Scrooge.

SCROOGE: Christmas? Bah humbug!

DARLA: Whoa! That's the last thing we need is an old humbug! Andy?

ANDY: Yo dog, I'd rather do the luge than vote for Ebenezer Scrooge.

RYAN: Silas, what do you say?

SILAS: Are you kidding? He's the perfect symbol for Christmas!

DARLA: Oh my goodness!

SILAS: I'm serious! Who isn't tired of the commercialism of Christmas? All those stupid TV specials? And that kid with the BB gun 24 hours straight?

Skits, Plays, and Dramas for Teens and Adults

DARLA: That's it! I'll be in my trailer!

[DARLA stands and exits.]

ANDY: Peace on earth and peace out!

[ANDY exits.]

SILAS: You're only mad because I'm right!

[SCROOGE exits. THE THREE KINGS enter.]

RYAN: We'll be back to find out what Silas has to say about these guys from the East.

[Theme music plays. Blackout.]

Missing Out at Christmas

by JOHN COSPER

Summary: A young couple, striving to have the perfect holiday, misses a dozen signs pointing them to the real story of Christmas.

Characters:

> PHIL—newlywed
> SUSAN—newlywed
> ERIN KING—friend of SUSAN
> RALPH KING—friend of SUSAN
> JOSEPH KING—friend of SUSAN

Setting: the mall

Props: shopping bags full of gifts

Costumes: winter clothes, tacky Christmas sweaters for PHIL and SUSAN

PHIL and SUSAN enter, laughing together, carrying shopping bags.

SUSAN: Well, we've done it. Our first year as a couple, and we've finished all our Christmas shopping.

PHIL: We got everything?

SUSAN: We took care of your folks, my folks, your brother, your sister and her husband and their kids, my sister and her hubby and her kids . . .

PHIL: What did we get your nieces?

SUSAN: The baby dolls with the drinking bottles, remember?

PHIL: And what did you get me?

SUSAN: *[giggles]* I'm not telling.

PHIL: So, it's 4:30 on Christmas Eve. What's on the agenda now?

SUSAN: Well, we have dinner at my folks, then opening gifts, and then the party at Elaine's. Presents in the morning for you and me, then lunch at your folks' place, dinner with my folks, and another party at the Daniels' house. What's wrong?

PHIL: Well, I don't know. It just seems like something's missing. We saw all the movies, right?

SUSAN: We watched *It's A Wonderful Life* last night, *Home Alone* on Thanksgiving, *Rudolph* was last week, *Christmas Vacation* is at my parent's place tonight, *Christmas Story* after lunch tomorrow.

PHIL: What about *Charlie Brown*?

SUSAN: It was on when you were out of town last week, but I taped it for you.

PHIL: Good. But, you know, I still think we've missed something in this season. I wonder what that could be?

[The KINGS enter, carrying shopping bags full of gifts.]

SUSAN: Oh my goodness! Look who it is!

PHIL: Who?

SUSAN: It's the three Kings!

PHIL: Who?

SUSAN: My old friends from high school—the King family.

ERIN: Hey, Susan!

SUSAN: Hey, you guys! Phil, these are my friends the Kings—Erin, Ralph, and Joseph.

PHIL: I remember you. You all came to the wedding.

ERIN: Good to see you again, Phil.

RALPH: Merry Christmas.

PHIL: Merry Christmas to you.

SUSAN: Wow, seems like forever since we last saw each other. What are you doing up here?

JOSEPH: The usual last minute Christmas shopping.

ERIN: Bearing gifts for the newborn King.

PHIL: Excuse me?

RALPH: Joseph and his wife had a baby last week.

SUSAN: Ohhhhh, Joseph, congratulations!

JOSEPH: Thank you.

ERIN: You should see him, Susan. He's the cutest thing.

SUSAN: That's so wonderful. And how's Mary, Joseph?

JOSEPH: Well, she had a few complications in delivery and had a rough day or two, but everything's stable now.

SUSAN: I'm so glad.

RALPH: Oh, you will never believe who's in town visiting.

SUSAN: Who?

RALPH: The Shepherds!

SUSAN: Rob and Diane?

ERIN: Yes!

SUSAN: Wow, I haven't seen them in forever.

JOSEPH: Yeah, they came to see the baby after they heard about him from Gabriel.

SUSAN: Gabriel Roberts? Wow, there's someone else I haven't seen in a while.

JOSEPH: Well the Shepherds came in last night. They're staying with us too.

ERIN: They tried to get a room at the Holiday Inn, but it's Christmas so there is no room in the inn.

SUSAN: I'd love to see them.

PHIL: Well, maybe we can stop by.

JOSEPH: Oh, please do, yes. We'll all be staying at Mom and Dad's.

SUSAN: Oh, the one off Bethlehem Road?

JOSEPH: Yeah, that's it.

RALPH: Right behind the Lone Star Steakhouse.

ERIN: The one with the big, bright star out front.

PHIL: That shouldn't be hard to find.

JOSEPH: Yeah, if you're coming from the east, just follow Bethlehem Road til you see the star.

PHIL: Sounds good.

ERIN: Well, we need to get going, but maybe we'll see you later?

JOSEPH: Drop by any time. We'll catch you later. Merry Christmas.

PHIL & SUSAN: Merry Christmas.

[The KINGS exit.]

SUSAN: Wow, that was great.

PHIL: What a nice family.

SUSAN: So did you think of what we're missing?

PHIL: No, I didn't. It's probably something so obvious, we'll kick ourselves later.

SUSAN: I wonder what it could be.

[They both think and then eyes widen. They look at each other and snap fingers in unison.]

PHIL & SUSAN: *[shouting]* Candy canes!

[Blackout.]

Between Two Mothers

by PAULA REED

Summary: This sketch looks into the plans MARY might have had for her newborn baby. *[Related Scripture: Luke 1:26-38; Matthew 1:18-25]*

Characters:

MARY—young woman

TERAH—young woman

Costumes: Bible-times costumes

MARY and TERAH walk in closely together, talking.

TERAH: I don't really know what to say! That the angel would deliver such a message to you is truly amazing!

MARY: I know it sounds incredible and it is amazing that the Lord would shine His favor upon me in such a way as this. It leaves me breathless and yet filled with wonder and joy. For me, a virgin, to be pregnant with the child of God is something I am just now beginning to grasp, but have yet to fully understand.

TERAH: I must confess it leaves me confused as well as a little frightened for you.

MARY: Frightened for me—why?

TERAH: Mary, surely you must know of the wagging tongues in our village. There are those who say you have brought disgrace to your family and should be stoned. That is why I had to find you and speak with you face-to-face.

MARY: Oh, Terah, you have always been such a loving and faithful friend! Please don't worry over me. While I may not know all of His plan, I am confident that the Lord will see me through, for the angel himself said to me, "Nothing is impossible with God."

TERAH: But what about Joseph? Does he believe that all you have told him is true?

MARY: He didn't at first—in fact he planned to break our betrothal quietly to save me from further shame and embarrassment. I believe he was deeply wounded thinking that maybe I had been with another man.

TERAH: And now?

MARY: He was also visited by a messenger of God and believes that what has been foretold will come to pass. He has vowed to honor our pledge and we will be married soon. Joseph is a righteous man, for God has chosen him to be the father of His own Son and I am honored to be his wife.

TERAH: Dear Mary, your faith has always been as deep as the sea. You are truly God's humble servant—no wonder you have found such favor with Him.

MARY: While I cannot fathom the mysteries of our Lord, I do believe and trust in His purpose for my life. And your words are very comforting to me, my friend. I will miss you while I am away visiting my cousin, Elizabeth.

TERAH: As I will miss you. *[shyly]* And when you return I will have a surprise for you as well!

MARY: A surprise? Terah, what is it? We have never kept secrets from one another—please tell me!

TERAH: Simon didn't want me to say anything just yet, but . . . I, too, am with child!

MARY: Terah! I am so happy for you and for Simon! And to think that we will carry our children together brings me such joy! This is wonderful news!

TERAH: We are so happy—our first child! We have such hopes and dreams for this little one. But tell me, Mary, what does the mother of the child of God hope for her son?

MARY: *[thoughtfully]* I suppose I am no different than you, Terah, or any other mother for that matter. But to think and dream about His future is more than my feeble mind can comprehend. Dare I think that I can shape the destiny of the Son of the Most High? He is conceived of the Holy Spirit but yet His life grows within me, a mere woman. I may choose His sandals, but the Lord will direct His steps. When He cries, I will dry His tears even though they will be the very tears of God; and when He laughs, I will dance with joy at the sound of His voice. I am not worthy of any of this, but I am willing, and I humbly accept God's precious gift given to me.

TERAH: But, surely, you must wonder of His future. For what do you suppose the angel meant when he said, "His kingdom will never end"? Forgive me, Mary, but you are as poor as I—we have not the means, or the resources, to build a village, let alone a kingdom.

MARY: What you say is true and of course I wonder—I wonder if His life will be marked with joy or with sorrow. I wonder what He will have to endure to bring salvation to our people as the prophets foretold many years ago. I do not know how the Lord intends to build His kingdom through His Son, Jesus—will it be with blood and tears or with power and might? I do not know what His future holds but somehow I know He holds our future. I do not know many things but I do know that I will love this baby boy and I will tenderly and lovingly care for this holy child of God.

TERAH: *[softly]* Perhaps that is all you need to know for now. You will be such a good mother.

MARY: As will you, Terah. And we will help each other when the nights are long and our days filled with the tasks of raising our children! But what about you, my friend? What do you dream for your unborn child?

TERAH: I hope that he will be healthy and strong and a kind and honest person. That he will remember the goodness of our Lord Jehovah and follow His commands. I pray that if there is a defining moment that changes his life, it will be for the good, not the bad. Of course, if he has a head for buying and selling like his father—that would be an added blessing!

MARY: *[laughing with her]* Are you already so convinced it is a son you carry?

TERAH: Simon desperately wishes for a son and has already chosen his name—if in fact it is a boy! He is to be called Judas—Judas Iscariot. Simon thinks it is a name of strength and power.

MARY: Judas it is then. May God bless you and Simon with a son and may he grow into your dreams for him.

TERAH: Who knows? Perhaps my son will serve your son, Jesus, in His new kingdom and together they will change all of history!

MARY: Maybe we go too far in our thinking, Terah! Perhaps our best response is to just trust in the creator to fulfill His promise as He determines. But now I must hurry and go see my cousin, Elizabeth. Take care, my friend, and I will see you soon.

TERAH: Goodbye, Mary, and may God be with you and Joseph in the days and months ahead.

[Blackout.]

What Child Is This?

by JOHN COSPER

Summary: MARY recalls the events that led up to her giving birth to Jesus and wonders why she was chosen and how she will live up to the calling.
Character:
   MARY—the mother of Jesus
Setting: Bethlehem
Costume: Bible-times costumes

MARY is at center stage.

MARY: Look at him. He's just the most precious thing, isn't he? I always knew he had a soft touch, but . . . the way he holds that baby is amazing. I don't think I've ever seen him wearing a face like that. Not even when he's holding me. I always knew Joseph would be a great father. I just never dreamed it would happen this way. *[looks up]* But no one but You could have dreamed up the year I've had. It began simply enough. Well, I say simply, but having an angel appear in your house is not an every day occurrence. "Greetings, you who are highly favored. The Lord is with you." I remember falling to my knees and at the same time pinching myself, thinking I was dreaming. I wasn't, of course, and the angel told me what was to happen. I would bear a son. He would be the Son of God, conceived by the Holy Spirit. "May it be to me as you have said," I consented. Not that I had any power over the situation. If anything, I might have suggested choosing a more noble or well to do woman for the job, but . . . I mean you don't question an angel, do you? I was excited, and ran to tell my cousin Elizabeth about it. She was bearing a promised child just as I was, a boy named John. But after that visit, reality set in. How was I going to tell Joseph? What would people think when they found out I was with child? And what would they do? Only a year earlier, another girl in Nazareth had become pregnant out of wedlock. She was taken outside town and stoned. I believed that you would protect me, but

. . . it didn't stop me from becoming very afraid. A few days after I was visited by the angel, I told Joseph. He just sat there, silent, not knowing what to say. I could tell part of him wanted to believe me, but . . . well, I understand why he couldn't. He left and I didn't see him for several days. I found out he was planning to break our engagement quietly, so as not to disgrace me. That told me that he really loved me, and it made it all that much harder to think of losing him. I needed my Joseph if I was to become a mother so young. You knew that and sent an angel to tell him the same news you told me. You also gave him our son's name: Jesus, the deliverer. The Messiah. Instead of a quiet divorce, we had a quiet wedding. And not a moment too soon, as I began to show almost immediately. Though nothing was ever said, I knew that the eyes on my belly in the market suspected that I had been pregnant before the wedding. So much gossip circulates in Nazareth anyway, and even the chance of such a scandal was too good for the people to pass up. Joseph shielded me from any potential embarrassment as much as he could. Often times he did the shopping and fetched water for us, things that normally only the women in town did, just to protect me. I wondered how he would do that when the time for the baby came. Turns out You had a plan in motion. The time for the birth approached, and the Roman government issued a decree for a census to be taken. I couldn't believe it. Nine months pregnant with Your child, and You wanted me to take to the road? The good part about the census was that I would not have to give birth under the suspicious eyes of the people of Nazareth. The hard part was the back of a donkey jostling me and my very full womb around on the rocky road into Bethlehem. My mom joked that it would be good for me, and would probably induce labor. Boy was she right. As if that wasn't enough, we had to settle for a stable versus a hotel room. Hardly the place I would choose for the Messiah to be born, and yet . . . well, You were there with me. I brought Your Son into the world in that tiny stable, laying out on a bed of hay. And now He sleeps in an animal trough converted into a makeshift cradle. In all the confusion and craziness, I nearly forgot exactly how all this began—with an angel and a promise. I was exhausted, tired, and wondered where You were in all this. Then came the shepherds, saying they too had seen angels. The angels told them the Messiah had been born, and when the shepherds saw my son—Your Son—they fell down and worshiped Him. And that was when it really hit me: as hard as these nine months have been, as intimidating as the gossip could get, I have never been more terrified than I am right now. I'm so young, Lord. And it's so soon for me to be having a family anyway. In so many ways, I'm still a child, and now, I'm responsible for another life. And not just any life, but the life of Your only Son! I've asked the question a hundred times and still can't find an answer. Why would You choose me? What qualities, what qualifications do I have that make me more remarkable than all the women in Israel? This is such a heavy burden to place on my shoulders, and yet You've done it, with absolute confidence and assurance. I think back time and time again to the angel. The warm look on his face. And the words he spoke, "For nothing is impossible with God." Does that really include making a child like me the woman to raise the Messiah? Who am I to teach Him the story of creation when He witnessed it? Who am I to teach Him the law of Moses when He was the one to author it? And will I be the one to tell Him of His destiny, that He will deliver Israel from oppression? How will I be able to discipline a child like Him? Or will that even be necessary? Will He be the one to chastise me and correct my actions when I sin? How will I explain to Him . . . how can I teach the immortal Son of God about death? So many questions. So few answers. But I guess for tonight, well, I don't have to know any of the answers, do I? Tonight He is a baby, so let Him rest. Let me rest as well. And please, please stay near me. I'm going to need all the strength and wisdom You can give me to fulfill the destiny You've given to me.

[Blackout.]

A Shepherd's Voice

by PAULA REED

Summary: Sometime after the shepherds had visited the manger on the first Christmas Eve, one SHEPHERD returns to the field where he tells of the evening's event to his son, AARON, who has met him there. *[Related Scripture: Luke 2:8-20; Micah 5:4-5]*

Characters:

    SHEPHERD—father of AARON, middle-aged man

    AARON—son of the SHEPHERD, teen male

Props: backdrop to resemble a starry-night sky, artificial trees/plants, rocks for scenery

Costumes: Bible-times costumes

SHEPHERD appears pacing back and forth, obviously full of excitement and wonder over what he has just seen and heard.

SHEPHERD: I wonder if this night will be remembered? Will the generations to come understand the significance of this holy night?

[AARON runs in to join him, breathless and excited.]

AARON: Papa! I came as fast as I could when I heard the news!

SHEPHERD: *[embracing AARON when he runs in]* Aaron, my son, I am so glad to see you! I have much to tell you! And you must listen carefully to what I am about to say. Never forget this night and what it means to you, to our people. Nothing will be the same after tonight.

AARON: *[asking rapid fire questions]* But, father, is it true? Has the Messiah really come to save us? Is He strong? How did He get here? *[questions continue as father interrupts]*

SHEPHERD: *[Laughing at his son's excitement, he leads him to a rock.]* Sit here, my child, and let me start at the beginning. This has been no ordinary night, I tell you! I, along with your uncles and cousins, was tending the sheep. Night had fallen, but, oh, what a night. The stars seemed to sparkle and dance against the black, velvet sky. But for the bleating of the sheep, all was calm and quiet. Out in the open fields, the crisp, cool wind caused us to gather around the fire where we huddled for warmth. Your cousin, Nathaniel, had just joined us after his watch over the flock in the eastern field. I was just getting ready to leave and take his place when a light shone all around us—a light so radiant that we fell to the ground and covered our faces to escape it. We were terrified! It was as if Yahweh parted the sky like a curtain and poured Heaven's light down upon us.

AARON: *[excitedly]* Then what, father?

SHEPHERD: Then, my child, an angel appeared to us and he spoke.

AARON: A *real* angel? What did he say?

SHEPHERD: He was very real, Aaron. His garment was a brilliant white, his body glowing. His face was so kind, so gentle, and yet his voice rang across the fields commanding respect and attention. Even the sheep were silent! Trembling, we bowed our heads, but our fear soon turned to joy when he said, "Do not be afraid. I bring you good news of great joy that will be to you; for all the people. Today in the town of David a Savior has been born; he is Christ the Lord. This will be a sign to you and you will find the baby wrapped in cloths lying in a manger." We turned to one another in amazement when suddenly there was an explosion of light and sound! The sky peeled open and a host of angels, mighty and glorious, joined with the angel singing and praising God. They sang, "Glory to God in the highest and on earth peace on whom his favor rests." Their voices filled the air with the sweetest, richest melody that man has ever heard. In complete awe and wonder, we lifted our faces and our hands, praising God with the angels. And then as quickly as they came, they left as the sky closed in around them. Our eyes had to adjust to the darkness once again, and we wondered aloud at what we had just witnessed.

AARON: So did you go, Papa—did you go see the baby?

SHEPHERD: We left the fields as fast as our feet could carry us and went into Bethlehem. And there, at the edge of the town, we found Him lying in a manger just as the angel said we would. We still couldn't believe that the Lord had brought this announcement to us, simple shepherds, but we knew we must be obedient and find the Christ child.

AARON: Tell me what you saw—what was it like?

SHEPHERD: When we first came to the stable, we were excited—all of us were talking at once about all that we had seen and heard. But something happened when we came to the manger and saw the babe wrapped in cloths and held by his young mother. Immediately a hush came over us and we were filled with a holy awareness. I have never felt anything like it before. We were hesitant at first, as we didn't want to intrude upon them or break the quietness of the moment. But the young mother, her name is Mary, and her husband, Joseph, beckoned us to come closer. And the closer we came to the Christ child the more we felt as if we were ushered into the very presence of the Lord Jehovah himself. We bowed in humble adoration, tears of joy streaming down our faces as our hearts accepted that we beheld our Messiah—the long awaited one! As I knelt before Him, His tiny, wrinkled hand, pushing through the hay and straw, touched mine, and I was filled with incredible peace.

AARON: I want to go to the stable too, Papa! But I still don't understand why He was born in a manger, instead of a palace.

SHEPHERD: I do not understand it myself, Aaron. I only know I saw and believed. Like most of our people, I had envisioned a mighty king and a vast army—someone who would conquer our oppressors with an iron hand. At the very least I imagined our Savior would be a rich and powerful ruler. I am only a simple shepherd, and we are the poorest of our people. And yet on this holy night, I feel as if I've been made rich because I've seen the Christ child. I dare not question Jehovah's plan for our salvation, and if it is found in the tenderness and gentleness of a baby, then so it shall be.

AARON: Did you take him a gift—a gift fit for a king?

SHEPHERD: I had nothing to offer Him but my faith and my trust. Somehow it seemed fit for our Redeemer—

AARON: [standing and tugging on his father] I can't wait to see Him, father! Will you take me now?

SHEPHERD: Yes, my son. And remember we must never forget this holy night. You must tell it to your children and your children's children. Come, let us go to the manger and worship our King!

[SHEPHERD and AARON exit. Blackout.]

Mary, on Jesus' Birth

by DIANA C. DERRINGER

Summary: The mother of Jesus reflects on God's use of the ordinary to accomplish His purpose.

Characters:

MARY—woman dressed in Bible-times costume

Setting: a stable in Bethlehem with a hay-filled manger set at one side of the stage

Props: long strip of muslin or other off-white cloth

Costumes: Bible-times costume

Mary is seated a few feet from the manger, slowly rolling the piece of cloth.

MARY: Traveling is always so difficult but especially when a baby is due. Joseph has been wonderfully patient about resting when necessary; his furrowed brow made me aware of how worried he was. When Bethlehem was finally in sight, instant relief spread over his face. Little did we realize the challenges that were still ahead. Because so many other travelers also had to register for the census in Bethlehem, we were unable to find a room anywhere. Thankfully, an innkeeper agreed for us to stay here with the animals. *[looking around]* Really, the accommodations are not bad at all. Joseph made a nice, comfortable spot for me to rest *[patting the space beside her]*, and the opportunity to lie down was wonderful. Just being off my feet, not having to dodge other travelers, and being able to sleep— what pleasure! It was not long, however, before my baby decided to make His presence known, in a big way. The pain of labor was definitely difficult, but what joy to see Jesus' little face the first time *[putting aside the cloth and holding out her hands]* and to count his 10 little fingers *[moving hands downward]* and 10 little toes. He was so beautiful it was overwhelming. After we wrapped Him in some cloths, we made a bed for Him in an animal trough. That was not exactly the sort of arrangement I expected to provide when I first learned that I was to be the mother of the Messiah, but then neither would I have expected to be chosen for this role. Yet here we are, *[gesturing with one hand]* not fancy but cozy and comfortable. Although it was not needed, Joseph and I received additional confirmation just a little bit ago that Jesus really is the promised one. Some shepherds from the surrounding fields came to worship Jesus. They told of angels appearing to proclaim Jesus' birth to them and providing directions to our location. Again, not the sort of people I would have anticipated to first receive word from God about the birth of our Lord. They were so excited; there was no doubt in my mind that the message would spread quickly once they left us. So here we are, poor people in poor circumstances, visited by poor and unclean men, with the hope of all the ages lying in a manger just a few feet away.

[Blackout.]

Skits, Plays, and Dramas for Teens and Adults